Praise for *Decolonizing Wealth*

"By anchoring the solutions to America's ills in the wisdom and knowledge of its original people, Edgar challenges all of us to analyze how our nation's history of racism and disenfranchisement has infected its financial and giving institutions."
—**Heather McGhee, Distinguished Senior Fellow, Demos**

"*Decolonizing Wealth* offers a refreshing and inspired look at how wealth can better serve the needs of communities of color and atone for the ways in which it has traditionally been used to inflict harm and division."
—**Kevin Jennings, President, Tenement Museum**

"Edgar has gone out on a limb to help lead us to a place of healing. He bravely calls out the power dynamics within the nonprofit and philanthropic sectors, particularly the white supremacy institutionally embedded into the system of nonprofit supplicant and philanthropic largesse."
—**Kathy Ko Chin, President and CEO, Asian & Pacific Islander American Health Forum**

"Finally, a Native perspective on how to heal internal systemic challenges. *Decolonizing Wealth* not only is an unflinching examination of today's philanthropic institutions and the foundations upon which they were built but also offers critical wisdom applicable to many sectors."
—**Sarah Eagle Heart (Lakota), CEO, Native Americans in Philanthropy**

"Edgar reinserts purpose and humanity into a philanthropic industry that has too often been driven by wealth accumulation, grant cycles, portfolios, and metrics."
—**John H. Jackson, President and CEO, Schott Foundation for Public Education**

"If you want to know how funders can redeem our souls, this book is a critical step in the right direction. Edgar is a courageous voice shaping a new era of activist grantmaking, one centered on achieving, not just studying opportunity and racial equity."
—**Eric K. Ward, philanthropist and Executive Director, Western States Center**

"Edgar's voice will help shape the future of a philanthropy that systemically reverses the toxic inequalities that threaten the very fabric of our human existence. It gives me hope for the soul of our sector."
—**Pia Infante, Co–Executive Director, The Whitman Institute**

"Charity and philanthropy rarely offer meaningful challenges to systems of white supremacy, patriarchy, and capitalism. *Decolonizing Wealth* is an important contribution to the grassroots struggles to transform society and shift the way we think about our relationship with money."
—**Jordan Flaherty, author of *No More Heroes***

"For charities and donors trying to shift the giving paradigm and channel resources in ways that are truly equitable, Edgar's ideas for solutions—based on Indigenous culture and traditions—couldn't come at a better time."
—**Nan Aron, President, Alliance for Justice**

"*Decolonizing Wealth* offers an arrow to pierce the status quo. While the heart of the revolution for justice is not dependent on philanthropic support, there can be a powerfully effective role for mindful philanthropy to respectfully contribute to the reimagining and actualization of a more just world for future generations."
—**Tia Oros Peters (Shiwi), Executive Director, Seventh Generation Fund for Indigenous Peoples**

"Nothing is more important to decolonize than money—without it, change is slower and harder and comes too late for too many people. Edgar Villanueva is a fresh voice in the money scene, one we should all heed."
—**Rinku Sen, author and strategist**

"Edgar has broken through the tired jargon of philanthropy-speak and written a fresh, honest, painful, and hopeful book, grounded in his own truths and Native traditions. He offers some radical thinking about what it would take to create a world in which power and accountability shifted and communities controlled the resources vital to their strength and futures."
—**Gara LaMarche, President, Democracy Alliance; former President, Atlantic Philanthropies; and former Vice President and Director of US Programs, Open Society Foundations**

DECOLONIZING
WEALTH

DECOLONIZING WEALTH

Indigenous Wisdom
to Heal Divides and Restore Balance

Edgar Villanueva

Foreword by Jennifer and Peter Buffett

BK

Berrett-Koehler Publishers, Inc.
a BK Currents book

Berrett-Koehler Publishers, Inc.
1333 Broadway, Suite 1000
Oakland, CA 94612-1921
Tel: (510) 817-2277; Fax: (510) 817-2278
www.bkconnection.com

ORDERING INFORMATION

Quantity sales. Special discounts are available on quantity purchases by corporations, associations, and others. For details, contact the "Special Sales Department" at the Berrett-Koehler address above.

Individual sales. Berrett-Koehler publications are available through most bookstores. They can also be ordered directly from Berrett-Koehler: Tel: (800) 929-2929; Fax: (802) 864-7626; www.bkconnection.com.

Orders for college textbook / course adoption use. Please contact Berrett-Koehler: Tel: (800) 929-2929; Fax: (802) 864-7626.

Distributed to the U.S. trade and internationally by Penguin Random House Publisher Services.

Berrett-Koehler and the BK logo are registered trademarks of Berrett-Koehler Publishers, Inc.

Printed in Canada

Berrett-Koehler books are printed on long-lasting acid-free paper. When it is available, we choose paper that has been manufactured by environmentally responsible processes. These may include using trees grown in sustainable forests, incorporating recycled paper, minimizing chlorine in bleaching, or recycling the energy produced at the paper mill.

Library of Congress Cataloging-in-Publication Data

Names: Villanueva, Edgar, author.
Title: Decolonizing wealth : indigenous wisdom to heal divides and restore
    balance / by Edgar Villanueva ; foreword by Jennifer and Peter Buffett.
Description: First edition. | Oakland, CA : Berrett-Koehler Publishers, Inc.,
    2018. | Includes bibliographical references and index.
Identifiers: LCCN 2018019438 | ISBN 9781523097890 (pbk.)
Subjects: LCSH: Income distribution--United States. | Wealth--United States.
    | Unjust enrichment--United States. | Restitution--United States. |
    Indians of North America--United States. | Slavery--United States. |
    Postcolonialism--United States.
Classification: LCC HC110.I5 .V55 2018 | DDC 339.2/20973--dc23
LC record available at https://lccn.loc.gov/2018019438

First Edition

26 25 24 23 22 21 20 19 18   10 9 8 7 6 5 4 3 2 1

Book producer: Linda Jupiter Productions
Text designer: Mayapriya Long, Bookwrights
Cover designer: Irene Morris

Copyeditor: Lunaea Weatherstone
Proofreader: Mary Kanable
Indexer: Paula C. Durbin-Westby

To the memory of my granddaddy, Johnson Lee Jacobs, Sr.,
who created a path to spirituality for many
and taught me the story of redemption.
I hope I'm making you proud.

"If we are going to heal, let it be glorious."
—Beyoncé

Contents

Foreword

Fortunate, privileged, blessed—we had always known we were all of these things, but 2006 took things to another level.

That was the year that Warren Buffett, Peter's father, bestowed on us a gift that would eventually total billions of dollars, to fund charitable work of our choosing. Despite Peter's famous last name, this sum of money was far beyond anything either of us had ever fathomed, much less controlled.

It was a responsibility with a weight we had never known. It meant we were suddenly expected to have all the answers. It meant we were invited into conversations with heads of state, investment managers, corporate leaders, entrepreneurs, and other big philanthropists, the global ruling elite, an overwhelmingly white and male crowd. These were the people who held forth on innovation, solutions, and progress. These were the people entrusted with leadership, whom investors think of as strategic, from whom the world expects great things.

The more we heard, the more we realized that these rooms full of wealthy and powerful white men could not possess the wisdom we sought. Far too often, they were searching for answers with their right hand to problems that they had created or contributed to with their left.

Those who had benefited most from the system of wealth consolidation were seen as the experts and the saviors of those who had been exploited and harmed by it. But why? In our own experience, assuming control of a vast amount of money had nothing to do with having all the answers. If there was one thing we were clear on, it was that we didn't have answers; all we could do was listen and practice humility. We devoted ourselves instead to an earnest search for fresh ideas that show unusual promise for significant impact.

Humility is something we could stand to see a lot more of among those of us who control the wealth of the world. Humility is not the same thing as modesty or false modesty. Humility is characterized by an accurate sense of self—assessing not just our weaknesses but also our privileges and strengths, being honest with ourselves about both. The root of the word is related to the soil, like the word "humus." Humility literally means being close to the ground.

This is where we find expertise and solutions, too: close to the ground, close to experience. The communities who have direct experience of an issue are by far the best experts on it.

Two other things that are etymologically close to the ground are the *radical*, which comes from "root" and the *Indigenous*, which means to be native to a place or born of a place.

Edgar Villanueva brings together all three of these things—an Indigenous, Native American voice that is simultaneously humble and radical. When we first met Edgar, we knew his leadership and writing would be a key to unlocking the stranglehold that the broken capitalist, patriarchal, and colonial systems have on our deeply divided country. Edgar calls us to dig deeper for different ways of being, rooted in love of humanity and the earth.

Again and again he asks us here to imagine: *What if?*

"Even just asking the question opens us to radically different possible realities and can lead to healing, to a greater sense of dignity and purpose," he writes.

What if we could use wealth to heal rather than cause further harm? *What if* funders, philanthropists, and entrepreneurs could help restore the earth? *What if* money was spent trying out concepts that shatter current structures and systems that have turned much of the world into one vast market?

Getting from "here" to "there" is rarely obvious or a straight line. But radical imagination—daring to ask *What if?*— is always part of the process.

Everything Edgar is saying feels fundamentally different—and fundamentally true. It is clear that his voice, and that of many other Native and marginalized leaders, illuminates a path forward, in the face of extreme inequality, violence, and greed.

Voices like Edgar's remind us that progress and unity can be found by trusting in the deep wisdom of local communities, rather than chasing expertise from outside. It demonstrates that true healing, and lasting justice, won't be discovered in the technological advancements of the future, but recovered in the time-tested wisdom found close to the ground. It offers the radical hope that money might be used as medicine, after all, to heal the trauma and wounds we all bear.

—Jennifer and Peter Buffett

What if Money Could Heal Us

This is a book for people who direct the flow of money. The more money you direct, the more this book is for you. You may be a philanthropist, an investor, or a funds manager; you may work for a foundation, a bank, or a community. You may be an "ordinary person" interested in the money invested through your pension or insurance. You may think of yourself as wealthy; maybe you would never use that word. Across the board, according to the numbers, you're more likely to be a white man, since more white men direct more of the flow of money.[1] But you may also be a woman, Black, brown, Indigenous, or anything else that is not a white man.

Whoever you are, you are welcome. As I will explain, in my own Native American belief system we are all relatives, literally all related to one another. We are also all infected with what I call the "colonizer virus," which urges us to divide, control, and exploit. Nowhere is the virus more symptomatic than in how we deal with wealth.

For some, reading this book may feel like I'm yanking off the Band-Aid. There may be moments of discomfort. I invite you to sit with it, in the understanding that I am motivated by love, and that things have been just as uncomfortable, if not really painful, for many of us, for a very long time.

In order to heal what hurts, to come back together as one human race, and to restore balance to the land, we need to decolonize wealth. This book will explain how we can begin to heal ourselves, using money as our medicine.

~~~~~

$127 million. That's how much money I have given away since 2005. Just under a million per month.

That's a significant sum for all but a handful of extremely wealthy people on the planet. It's even more astonishing given that I grew up in poverty. My people are dirt poor. They hail from Robeson County, North Carolina, the third poorest county in the United States, where more than a third of folks live on less than $15,000 per year, including most of my extended family. Yet I've made close to $130 million in philanthropic gifts. If that were 1.3 percent of my income—the average annual percentage given as donations by the super-wealthy[2]—I'd be earning around $750 million every year.

I would be, that is, if that money were my own. As it happens, I am that rare phenomenon: a Native American working in the field of philanthropy. Those millions are other people's money, entrusted to my hands.

~~~~~

The field of philanthropy is a living anachronism.

It is (we are) like a stodgy relative wearing clothes that will never come back in fashion. It is adamant that it knows best, holding tight the purse strings. It is stubborn. It fails to get with the times, frustrating the younger folks. It does not care.

It is (we are) like a mansion with neoclassical columns and manicured lawns staffed with butlers and maids who pass silver trays of tiny tasteless nibbles (*pigs in blankets, angels on horseback, anyone?*) to guests wearing tailcoats and bustles, as a string quartet plays tunes written centuries ago. No one's voice rises over a certain decibel, no one jokes, no one's words call attention to the ludicrous and unsustainable farce that is the entire scene.

It is (we are) a period play, a costume drama, a fantasy of entitlement, altruism, and superiority. Far too often, it creates (we create) division and suffering rather than progress and healing.

It is (we are) a sleepwalking sector, white zombies spewing the money of dead white people in the name of charity and benevolence.

It is (we are) colonialism in the empire's newest clothes.

It is (we are) racism in institutional form.

Philanthropy moves at a glacial pace. Epidemics and storms hit, communities go under water literally and metaphorically, Black and brown children get shot dead or lose their youth inside jail cells, families are separated across continents, women are abused and beaten and raped, all of Rome burns while we fiddle with another survey on strategies, another study on impact.

Other sectors feel the heat of competition. Not us. We politely nod at the innovations of the business sector; it takes us a half-century to implement one of them. We indulge those who say that diversity is important by conducting several decades of analyses, hiring consulting groups with absurd price tags. We publish reports. We create a task force and debate mightily over what to call it. We do not actually change, not more than superficially.

This is philanthropy. It is (we are) the family that embarrasses me and infuriates me. But it's still my family, my relations, and I believe in redemption. It's from the place of calling this family to a better self that I write.

Philanthropy, honey, it's time for an intervention.

~~~

Most critiques of philanthropy point the accusing finger at things like funding priorities, grantmaking decision processes, the tax code, and payout percentages. As far as I'm concerned, a focus on reforming this stuff is certainly valid, but ultimately about as effective as rearranging the deck chairs on the *Titanic*. Why? Because those are mere symptoms of a virus that has pervaded every aspect, every cell, every interaction. What remains unexamined with those kinds of reforms are frank conversations about where that wealth came from, why it's held back from public coffers, how it's invested as an endowment, and who gets to manage, allocate, and spend it.

My central argument is that what ails philanthropy at its core is colonialism. Almost without exception, funders reinforce the colonial division of Us vs. Them, Haves vs. Have Nots, and mostly white saviors and white experts vs. *poor, needy, urban, disadvantaged, marginalized, at-risk people* (take your pick of euphemisms for people of color). The statistics speak for themselves: *92 percent of foundation CEOs are white,*[3] *89 percent of foundation boards are white,*[4] *while only 7 to 8 percent of foundation funding goes specifically to people of color.*[5] Philanthropy is the savior mentality in institutional form, which instead of helping—its ostentatiously proclaimed intent—actually further divides and destabilizes society.

Part One of this book, "Where It Hurts," recounts my journey into the heart of philanthropy, past the field's glamorous, altruistic facade, into its shadows. I drill down to the core of the affliction, uncovering white supremacy, the savior mentality, and internalized oppression.

Yet while my own experience is centered in philanthropy, the same dynamics basically hold true across what I call the loans-to-gifts spectrum: Bank loans. Venture capital. Municipal bonds. Even social and ethical finance, impact investments, and humanitarian aid. Here the statistics are equally dismal: *The management of financial services is 81 percent white,*[6] *86 percent of venture capitalists are white,*[7] *as are more than 96 percent of angel investors.*[8] *On the receiving side, loans are denied to 42 percent of minority-owned firms, but denied to only 16 percent of white-owned firms.*[9] *A measly 1 percent of VC funding goes to African American and Latino entrepreneurs.*[10]

To sum it up: when it comes to getting or giving access to money, white men are usually in charge, and everyone else has to be twice (or more) as good to get half (or less) as much. All the institutions along the loans-to-gifts spectrum—I'll use the term "funders" to encompass them all—are "ivory towers," by which I mean institutions of racism and division. All these funders exist to preserve the wealth and privilege of a few, to separate them from the rest of us. Most employ money in the name of division, to reinforce fear, greed, and envy.

Now, some will say that it's "just the economy, stupid," the natural outcome of an ideology that puts the welfare of the free market and the rights of corporations before the welfare and rights of people. But I say that those who would focus the blame on the system of capitalism or neoliberalism are obscuring the real root of the problem. As Malcolm X said, "You can't have capitalism without racism."[11]

Since at least the 1400s, white supremacy has been the justification for colonization, the conquest and exploitation of non-European lands, backed by a claim of divine sanction. European white imperialism spent centuries marching around the world, using whatever means necessary to amass and consolidate resources and wealth. Now, adding insult to injury, those who were stolen from or exploited to make that wealth—Indigenous people, people of African descent, and many other people of color—must apply for access to that wealth in the form of loans or grants; we must prove ourselves worthy. We are demeaned for our lack of resources, scrutinized, and often denied access after all.

The tactics of colonization violate us and leave us traumatized, over generations, to this very day.

Yet there's a silver lining in this cataclysm. All of us who have been forced to the margins are the very ones who harbor the best solutions for healing, progress, and peace, by virtue of our outsider perspectives and resilience. When we reclaim our share of resources, when we recover our places at the table and the drawing board, we can design our healing. We can create new ways of seeking and granting access to money. We can return balance to the world by moving money to where the hurt is worst.

To paraphrase Maya Angelou: Once we know better, we need to do better.

Money as Medicine

For most people, medicine is something used to treat or cure a disease, often a man-made drug or sometimes an herb. Sometimes it refers to the whole field of *medicine*: hospitals, pharmacies, doctors, and so on. In Native traditions, however, *medicine* is a way of achieving balance. An Indigenous medicine person doesn't just heal illnesses—he or she can restore harmony or establish a state of being, like peacefulness. Medicine people live and practice among the people; access to them is constant and unrestricted. And the practice of medicine is not just limited to the hands of medicine people: everyone is welcome to participate. Engaging with medicine is a part of the experience of daily life. Traditionally, Indigenous people don't wait to be out of balance before they turn to medicine.

In the Indigenous worldview, many kinds of things can be medicine: a place, a word, a stone, an animal, a natural phenomenon, a dream, a life event like a coffee date with a friend, or even something that seems bad in the moment like the loss of a job. Have you ever looked back at your life and thought, "That was the best thing that could have ever happened to me"? That was medicine. In order for something or someone to serve as medicine, it only needs to be filled with or granted a kind of mystical or spiritual power. Anyone can find and use medicine, just by allowing your intuition and feelings to determine whether something can serve as medicine. You listen for its sacred power; you don't force it.

You don't choose the medicine, the elders say, it chooses you.

It has taken me a long, long time (patience is a virtue in Indian country) to accept that the medicine that has chosen me is money. Because, I mean, money? Come on. Money corrupts. Money is dirty, even filthy. Money is the root of all evil, doesn't the Bible say that?

But what is money but a way to measure value, to facilitate exchange? And what is exchange but a type of relationship between people? Money is a proxy for the sweat we spent on growing food, sewing clothes, assembling electronics, coding apps, creating entertainment, researching and developing innovations, etc. It's just a stand-in for the materials we used, the services granted, the responsibility shouldered. Money is a tool to reflect the obligations people develop to each other as they interact. It's "the measure of one's trust in other human beings," as anthropologist David Graeber writes in his comprehensive book *Debt*.[12]

Materially, it's a bit of nickel, zinc, copper. It's a little linen, mostly cotton, some ink. It's basically Kleenex adorned with dead presidents. Actually, today mostly it's a series of zeros and ones. Bytes, data on screens. Imaginary. Harmless.

And in fact, the Bible doesn't say money's the root of all evil. It says the *love* of money is the root of all evil—in other words, when we let it be more important than life, relationships, and humanity.

I'm not saying there aren't problems with money when it's hoarded, controlled, used to divide people, to oppress and dominate. But that's not the money's fault. Inherently it's value-neutral. Humans have used money wrongfully. We've made money more important than human life. We've allowed it to divide us. That *is* a sin. We forget that we humans made money up out of thin air, as a concept, a tool for a complex society, a placeholder for aspects of human relations. We forget that we gave money its meaning and its power.

Money is like water. Water can be a precious life-giving resource. But what happens when water is dammed, or when a water cannon is fired on protesters in subzero temperatures? Money should be a tool of love, to facilitate relationships, to help us thrive, rather than to hurt and divide us. If it's used for sacred, life-giving, restorative purposes, it can be medicine.

Money, used as medicine, can help us decolonize.

Seven Steps to Healing

In Part Two of this book, "How to Heal," I offer my thoughts on what we need to do to decolonize the institutions and processes around money. Across American history and through the present day, the accumulation of wealth is steeped in trauma. The process of healing from that trauma is central to decolonization. Acknowledging our woundedness is key. This is not just for individuals; institutions can also engage in the Seven Steps to Healing:

1. **Grieve:** We have to stop and feel the hurts we've endured.

2. **Apologize:** We must apologize for the hurts we've caused.

3. **Listen:** We must acknowledge the wisdom of those excluded and exploited by the system, who possess exactly the perspective and wisdom needed to fix it.

4. **Relate:** We need space to share our whole selves with each other and understand we don't have to agree in order to respect each other.

5. **Represent:** We must build whole new decision-making tables, rather than setting token places at the colonial tables as an afterthought.

6. **Invest:** We need to put ALL our money where our values are.

7. **Repair:** We must use money to heal where people are hurting, and stop more hurt from happening.

These steps aren't necessarily linear. Certain steps may need to be revisited, and the entire process may need to be repeated. In this way, it's more of a circular or spiral process. Like any clever virus, the colonizer mindset keeps mutating and adapting, so in order to heal fully, we will need to be vigilant and get booster shots.

This is not a silver bullet solution. There is no quick fix for the complexity of colonization. Decolonization is a process with roles for everyone involved, whether you're rich or poor, funder or recipient, victim or perpetrator. It may not feel like we're moving forward at all, during certain phases of healing. Patience and grit are required.

In fact, as you may have already noticed, I don't really do quick fixes: I tell stories. Hello, I'm a Native American! Storytelling, ideally spiced up with a bit of humor, is how we transmit wisdom. Patience is a virtue in Indian country. A lot of books on wealth and finance offer fast-food-style delivery of sound-bites and easy takeaways. Who are those books written by? More often than not, they are not by people who look like me. When someone other than a mainstream white expert is in charge of delivering value and knowledge, the experience is different. I come from a long line of Native storytellers and Southern storytellers. Listening to our stories is part of the decolonization process.

In creating this book, I had the honor and the pleasure of collecting stories from dozens of leaders from foundations, community organizations, and financial institutions. Most of them were Indigenous people and people of color; a handful were white folks. I asked them to speak candidly about the dynamics of race and power that they encounter in their work with money, and I asked them to share ideas for how we could decolonize wealth. Because their frank honesty could cause problems for them in their workplace, many chose to be quoted anonymously. I am incredibly grateful for those conversations, which deepened my analysis and furthered my thinking about the relationship between wealth and trauma.

All my relations—*Mitakuye Oyasin*, as the Lakota say, meaning we are all related, connected, not only to each other humans but to all the other living things and inanimate things and the planet, and also the Creator. The principle of All My Relations means that everyone is at home here. Everyone has a responsibility in making things right. Everyone has a role in the process of healing, regardless of whether they caused or received more harm. All our suffering is mutual. All our healing is mutual. All our thriving is mutual.

PART ONE

Where It Hurts

It is true that the first part of this book consists of mostly dark, painful stories, stories of what people endure to gain access to money, stories of the twisted things people do once they have access to money and the power it confers. My own journey through the world of philanthropy forms the backbone, leading to observations about wealth, the colonizer virus, and trauma. Some may say it's tiresome to dwell on the hurt—after all, there's a relentless (if artificial) drive to *Stay Positive!* in America, to focus only on solutions—yet an essential step in the process of decolonization is hearing out the painful stories of the colonized and the exploited, respectfully and with an open heart.

~~~

The chapters in Part One are named for elements in a slave plantation. As token people of color working within the field of philanthropy, one of our regular water cooler conversations over the years, held in hushed voices, revolves around the analogy of a plantation. The people with the least power are those seeking funding—the field hands: begging for scraps, given no dignity and treated with no respect. One step up, people of color working in philanthropy are the house slaves, because we get to be close to the power and the privilege. We benefit from our position in all kinds of ways. Different slaves behave differently once they get inside the master's house. Some help those who are still out in the fields. But others take on the characteristics of the master and lord it over those less fortunate. They do whatever it takes to keep their own lucky position intact and unthreatened. Then there are the overseers, usually a white man, but occasionally a slave promoted to the position. Granted, they are in a tough position, under pressure from the master to squeeze as much profit from the slaves as possible, but they are infamous for indifference, delusions of grandeur, and, at worst, cruelty. The overseer in a foundation might be its CEO or executive director.

The plantation metaphor implicitly raises the question of the "master's tools," a reference to the poet and civil rights activist Audre Lorde's declaration: "The master's tools will never dismantle the master's house."[1] In other words, given the level of trauma caused by the colonizer virus and wealth consolidation, can funders actually support transformational change? The master's tools, as I view them, are not money—the tools are anything corrupted to serve the aims of exploitation and domination. If money is an inherently neutral force, as I described in the introduction, then it can also be used for good, as medicine, as I will explore in Part Two.

There is a folktale about a serpent that once upon a time was plaguing a village. The serpent had devoured many of the villagers, including children, and everyone lived in fear of its next attack. A flute player who was still among the living decided something must be done. He packed a bundle of food and a knife, and he went to the edge of the village and began playing his flute. As he expected, the music drew the serpent to him, and in one bite the serpent swallowed the flute player. Inside the serpent's stomach it was dark, but the flute player pulled out his knife and cut away a little of the serpent's stomach and ate it. Bit by bit, he cut away the serpent's flesh from the inside. This went on for some time, until finally the flute player reached the serpent's heart. When he cut it out, the serpent died, and the flute player crawled out of the serpent and returned to the village, bringing along the serpent's heart to show everyone so they would know they no longer had reason to be afraid.

I see it as a story about grappling with collective trauma. We have to enter into the darkness of it. It can't be dealt with from the outside. We have to go inside, despite our resistance, and allow ourselves to feel swallowed up and surrounded by it. It might seem like the pain will never end and there is no way out of it, but bit by bit we come to the heart of the matter. The flute player had prepared himself for a prolonged reckoning. Some kinds of grappling, for especially deep wounds, are lifelong projects. If we do not reckon with it, however, if we carry around unresolved grief, we will spend our lives plagued by the serpent. When we finally get to the heart of the matter, we can emerge lighter and ready to build something new.

CHAPTER ONE

Stolen and Sold

How notions of separation and race resulted in colonization and trauma

Who's your people? That's the first question Lumbee Indians ask when we meet someone new, as if we're working out a massive imaginary family tree for humanity in our heads and need to place you on the appropriate limb, branch, or twig. We even sell a T-shirt that has that printed on it: "Who's your people?"

I throw people off with my Latino-sounding last name, which came from my non-biological father, who was in fact Filipino. He was in my mom's life, and therefore in my life, for a brief moment between the ages of zero and two. When I'm with other Lumbees I have to mention the last names of my grandfather and grandmother, Jacobs and Bryant, so they know where to place me in the Lumbee family tree. A Lumbee will keep an ear out for our most common surnames, like Brooks, Chavis, Lowry, Locklear. As soon as you say you're related to these families, the stories unfold: *I knew your great-grandfather. I knew your auntie.* There's always a connection.

If you've never met a Native American in person before, you might be saddled with some common misconceptions about me. I have never lived in a teepee. I've never even lived on a reservation. I can't survive in the wilderness on my own. I can't kill or skin a deer. Shoot, I can't even build a fire. No, I didn't get a free education (still paying off those loans!), and yes, I pay taxes.

It wasn't until my late twenties that I really began the process of deeply connecting with my Native heritage. There were three main reasons for this: One, I'm an urban Indian. At least half to three-quarters of us are. Note, "urban" doesn't necessarily mean we live in cities; it's a term that refers to all Indians who do not live on reservations. And yes, I use the terms "Native American" and "(American) Indian" interchangeably. Unless you're an Indian too, you're probably better off sticking with "Native American" just to keep things simple.

Two: I've spent the majority of my adult life working in philanthropy, basically the whitest, most elite sector ever.

Three: I'm Lumbee.

The people known today as Lumbee are the survivors of several tribes who lived along the coast of what is now North Carolina. Those ancestors were the first point of contact for the Europeans, in the late 1500s. So we have had nearly 500 years of interaction with the settlers. Contrast this with some of the West Coast tribes, for many of whom the experience of colonization has been going on for just 200-some years, less than half the time. My people have been penetrated by and exposed to whiteness for a long, long time—longer than any other North American Native community. We assimilated to survive. The fact that any shred of anything remotely appearing to be Native exists among us is really a miracle.

"Resilience" has become a trendy word in conversations about business, insurance, and climate: let me tell you, my people really have a corner on resilience.

Originally Sioux-, Algonquin-, and Iroquois-speaking people, today Lumbees have no language to call our own, although we have a distinctive dialect on top of the southern North Carolina accent. We have so fully embraced Christianity that when you go to apply for or renew your tribal membership card, you are asked which church you attend. While we maintain our notion of tribal sovereignty, we are pretty thoroughly colonized.

There are people who deny that Lumbees are Native at all, as if a group of opportunists just came together to make this tribe up because they wanted to get some government money. Honestly, that's ridiculous. All you have to do is go to Robeson County, North Carolina, where there are 60,000 people concentrated who definitely are not quite white or Black. Some of them look as stereotypically Indian as Sitting Bull, like my maternal grandfather did. Lumbee physical characteristics are on a spectrum of presenting white to presenting Black because the area historically has been a third, a third, a third—Lumbee, Black, and white—and there has been some intermingling over the last half millennium. In fact, the most probable fate of the famous Lost Colony of Roanoke—the group of English settlers led by Sir Walter Raleigh who arrived in 1584—is that they didn't disappear at all. They just got hungry and needed help, and the Native coastal Indians, my ancestors, took them in and integrated them. There have been linguistic studies on the British influences within the Lumbee dialect that further support that theory.[1]

Other Native tribes give Lumbees a hard time because of anti-Black racism. Indians elsewhere in the country have said things to me like, "Oh, you guys are not really Indian. You play hip-hop at your pow wows" (which is not true!). Or they've said we're not Indian because we're not fully recognized by the federal government. There's such a scarcity mentality—part of the legacy of the colonizers' competitive mindset—that there are Indians who fear there will be fewer federal resources paid out to them if more unrecognized Indians receive federal recognition.

It was only in 1956 that the U.S. Congress recognized Lumbees as Indians by passing the Lumbee Act, but the full benefits of federal recognition were not ensured in the act, and to this day we are still fighting for the federal legislation that would do so. There are six tribes in North Carolina, and only one, the Eastern Band of the Cherokee Nation, is federally recognized. Any of us could be unrecognized tomorrow. Federal recognition is given and taken away by the stroke of a pen. There have been tribes who were granted federal recognition by one administration until the next president who came in took it away—this happened to the Duwamish Tribe in Seattle.[2] We're all subject to someone who is not an Indian himself (it's usually a him) calling those shots.

When I was a child growing up in Raleigh, North Carolina, in the 1980s, official forms had boxes for white, Black, and Other. Until the migration of Latinos into the state in the 1990s, and later the Asians who came when Research Triangle Park really took off, Natives were usually the only people in the Other box. I always had to check the Other box. For the most part, that was the extent of my Native identity, because no one was stirring up Native pride or celebrating Lumbee heritage in my school. My family was more focused on survival.

Being Native American inherently involves an identity crisis. We're the only race or ethnicity that is only acknowledged if the government says we are. Here we are, we exist, but we still have to prove it. Anyone else can say they are what they are. No one has to prove that they're Black or prove that they're Latino. There are deep implications to this. The rates of alcoholism, substance abuse, and suicide are linked to this fundamental questioning of our identity. We exist in the Other box. To try and feel safe inside that box, and then be told you've got to prove your right to be in that box, that the box itself is under threat, is deeply demoralizing.

My identity as a Native American is complicated. It's been a long journey to decolonize myself and connect more deeply with my Indigenous heritage. Still, it's the bedrock foundation of my identity. If I were a tree, my Native identity would be my core, the very first ring.

Unpacking Colonization

Colonization seems totally normal because the history books are full of it—and because to this day many colonizing powers talk about colonization not with shame but with pride in their accomplishments—it's so strange. Conquering is one thing: you travel to another place and take its resources, kill the people who get in your way, and then go home with your spoils. But in colonization, you stick around, occupy the land, and force the existing Indigenous people to *become you*. It's like a zombie invasion: colonizers insist on taking over the bodies, minds, and souls of the colonized.

Who came up with this, and why?

Without going too deep into the details of humanity's evolution (there are other great books for that),[3] the concept of colonization followed the trend that seems to have begun when humans first became farmers and began managing, controlling, and "owning" other forms of life—plant and animal (this horrifying word, "livestock"). Conceptually, this required that humans think of themselves as separate from the rest of the natural world.

This was the beginning of a divergence from the Indigenous worldview, which fundamentally seeks not to own or control, but to coexist with and steward the land and nonhuman forms of life. As the philosopher Derek Rasmussen put it: *"What makes a people indigenous? Indigenous people believe they belong to the land, and non-indigenous people believe the land belongs to them."*[4] It's not that Indigenous people were or are without strife or violence, but their fundamental worldview emphasizes connection, reciprocity, a circular dynamic.

It's important to remember that a worldview is a human creation. It's not our destiny. It's not inevitable. Even though it came close to disappearing entirely as the separation worldview took hold and became dominant over several centuries, the Indigenous worldview persisted.

The separation worldview goes like this, on an individual level but also at every level of complexity:

The boundaries of my body separate me from the rest of the universe. I'm on my own against the world. This terrifies me, and so I try to control everything outside myself, also known as the Other. I fear the Other, I must compete with the Other in order to meet my needs. I always need to act in my self-interest, and I blame the Other for everything that goes wrong.

Separation correlates with fear, scarcity, and blame, all of which arise when we think we're not together in this thing called life. In the separation worldview, humans are divided from and set above nature, mind is separated from and elevated above body, and some humans are considered distinct from and valued above others—us vs. them—as opposed to seeing ourselves as part of a greater whole.

This fundamentally divisive mindset led to an endless number of categories by which to further divide up the world and then rank them, assigning to one side the lower rank, the lesser power. So the rational took its place and lorded over the emotional, male over female, expert over amateur, and so on. In every sector, the very structure and approach of organizations also reflected a divisive, pigeonholing, and ranking mindset.

The separation-based economy exploits natural resources and most of the planet's inhabitants for the profit of a few. It considers the earth an object, separate from us, with its resources existing solely for human use, rather than understanding the earth as a living biosphere of which we are just one part. Money, of course, has been used and is still constantly used to separate people— most fundamentally, into Haves vs. Have Nots.

Separation-based political systems create arbitrary nation-states with imaginary boundaries. Their laws and institutions oppress some groups and privilege others. Leaders and experts are considered a special breed, set apart from the common person; all the important choices are up to them. The separation-based political conversation revolves around the questions: *Whom should we fear?* and *Whom should we blame?*

Most damaging of all, a long line of mostly white male bullies and sociopaths took the concept of separation and used it to justify oppression, slavery, and colonization by "scientifically" claiming the inferiority of Africans and Indigenous people, among other Others. And so we got to white supremacy.

~~~~

I use the term "white supremacy" instead of "racism" because it explicitly names who in the system benefits and—implicitly—who bears the burden. One of the tactics of domination is to control the language around the perpetrator's bad behavior. To call the phenomenon "racism" makes it abstract and erases explicit mention of the one who profits from the dynamic. So when I say "white supremacy" it doesn't just mean the KKK and Identity Evropa and other hate groups.

White supremacy is a bizarre mythology created by people with pale skin. It asserts that paler people deserve more—more respect, more resources, more opportunity—for no reason beyond the utterly arbitrary and ultimately meaningless pigmentation of their skin. It says that pale people make the important decisions, while people of color pay the price. Pale people define what is normal; they make the rules. Whiteness is the default, the standard, the norm: when it goes without saying what someone's ethnic background is, it's because they are pale. Pale people fill the airwaves, screens, and history books with their stories, until it is hard to find heroes and role models who are not pale.

"This system rests on the historical and current accumulation of structural power that privileges, centralizes, and elevates white people as a group," writes Robin DiAngelo,[5] the whiteness studies professor who also coined the term "white fragility," which refers to the discomfort and resistance white people often express when these issues are raised. Fragile or not, the not just historical but present-day evidence is hard to dispute. DiAngelo again: "If, for example, we look at the racial breakdown of the people who control our institutions, we see that in 2016–2017:

Congress: 90% white

Governors: 96% white

Top military advisers: 100% white

President and vice president: 100% white

Current POTUS cabinet: 91% white

People who decide which TV shows we see: 93% white

People who decide which books we read: 90% white

People who decide which news is covered: 85% white

People who decide which music is produced: 95% white

Teachers: 83% white

Full-time college professors: 84% white . . ."[6]

Given that white people currently constitute only 60 percent of American citizens, you can see how far out of proportion those statistics are. Since the Trump election, the "whitelash" (per CNN commentator Van Jones) that followed our first Black president, and the resurrection of emboldened racism across the country, many of us feel this imbalance is only going to get worse.

Vanessa Daniel, executive director of the Groundswell Fund, calls the dynamic "the hubris of white supremacist conquest and imperialism and its insatiable thirst for total dominance over nature, over people of color, over anyone who is not white, Christian, cisgender, male, and rich. It has been a termite-like force that throughout history has eviscerated all in its path. . . ."[7]

Only recently has white supremacy begun to be called out. Its invisibility and taken-for-grantedness has been part of its enduring power. "If we can't identify it, we can't interrupt it," says DiAngelo.[8] In a world of white supremacy, white people are considered credible, the experts and authorities, while non-white people are often dismissed as untrustworthy and unreliable. When over decades the police, courts, banks, schools, and other parts of society regularly ignore, exploit, and harm non-white people, yet these incidents are largely denied, excused, or blamed on the victims, without being properly investigated, before disappearing from the accounts of history or the evening news or the general discourse: this is white supremacy. The humanity of certain people is made invisible.

At its height in the early 1920s (not very long ago!), the British Empire governed close to a fifth of the world's population and a quarter of the world's total land.[9] When in 2014 a poll among British citizens finds that 59 percent feel that their colonial activities are a source of pride, outnumbering those who feel colonization was a source of shame by three to one, that is white supremacy. When half of those polled state they believe the countries that were colonized were better off for being colonized, that's white supremacy, alive and kicking, in the twenty-first century.[10]

That there is widespread ambivalence today among the citizens of colonizing powers about whether or not colonization was a good thing is deeply offensive. Make no mistake: colonization is an atrocity, a close relative of genocide.

Divide, Control, Exploit

As far back as the 1400s, white supremacy, often in the name of Christianity, was employed to justify colonization—the conquest and exploitation of non-European lands—by claiming the inferiority of Africans and Indigenous people. The Christian Doctrine of Discovery specified that the entire world was under the jurisdiction of the pope, as God's representative on earth. Any land not under the sovereignty of a Christian ruler could be possessed on behalf of God. European colonizers sailed around the world taking stuff that didn't belong to them, asserting it was their God-given right to do so.

Academics who study colonization distinguish between external or exploitation colonization—in which the focus is on extracting goods like tea, silk, or sugar, or resources like human labor, coltan, or oil, in order to increase the wealth and power of the colonizer—and internal colonization, which seeks to manage and control people inside the borders of the empire, using tools like schooling, policing, segregation, surveillance, and divestment. These two kinds of colonialism can and often do coexist. Violence and exploitation are always part of the process. The mantra of colonizers is *divide, control,* (and above all) *exploit.*

In many countries around the world, the colonizers came, wreaked their havoc, and at some point left, sometimes after uprisings and independence movements succeeded in pushing them out. In America, however, they stayed. This is known as settler colonialism. Manifest Destiny, the rallying cry for westward expansion of the United States, was the Doctrine of Discovery updated for the nineteenth century.

In order to lay claim to land that did not belong to them, settlers had to erase everyone and everything that came before. They rewrote history to legitimize their actions. They had to find a way to justify their atrocious behavior, by claiming to be more deserving, more civilized, and superior to the original inhabitants, the First Nations. The settlers claimed their god granted them the right. And to be clear: *settlers cannot be considered immigrants* because immigrants are expected to obey the laws of the land when they arrive, while settlers make their own new laws of the land.

In all scenarios, colonization has deep, long-lasting impacts on the colonized, the natives, but settler colonialism makes things much, much messier. The Tunisian author Albert Memmi wrote: "It is not easy to escape mentally from a concrete situation, to refuse its ideology *while continuing to live with its actual relationships.*"[11] What makes it even more complicated in the United States is that, over time, the white settlers brought slaves and later attracted low-wage workers—many of them people of color—who all were hurt and exploited, yet who were technically also settlers from the Indigenous perspective.

The settlers caused death, disease, diaspora, and cultural subjugation of Native communities. They systematically suppressed our Native governance and sovereignty. They systematically delegitimized and stamped out our traditional, holistic ways of understanding, learning, and knowing. Forced removals traumatized Natives by severing us from the lands that contained the plants and animals we needed to sustain the physical, mental, cultural, and spiritual health of our communities. Our lands also contained the bones of our ancestors and the keys to our traditional ways of life.

When all these efforts and policies failed to extinguish us, the settlers launched the era of "boarding schools," separating Native children from their families and cultures, cutting off our hair, forbidding us to speak our languages, forcing us to act white. *Divide, control, exploit.*

Honestly, it's amazing that we survived at all.

These atrocities took place over hundreds of years, depending on where the Native community was located. Remember that my people were the first point of contact for the Europeans in the late 1500s and thus have nearly 500 years of experience with the settlers, whereas for the Natives of California, the experience of colonization has been going on for just about 200 years. This means that for many California Indians, the traumas experienced by their ancestors remain quite alive in community memory. At every gathering of Natives I attend, there are elders who as children experienced being ripped away from their families and homes and being forced to submit to indoctrination in white boarding schools. The horrors are that fresh.

~~~

Beginning in the 1960s, an era of Indigenous activism and tribal self-determination led to major reforms in policies directed at Native nations and Indigenous people in the United States, which coincided with the civil rights movement. The reforms included the Indian Child Welfare Act, the Native American Graves Protection and Repatriation Act, the American Indian Religious Freedom Act, and the Indian Self-Determination and Education Assistance Act—all of which provided much clearer federal acknowledgement of, and support for, tribal sovereignty, as well as self-determination in policies affecting our health, safety, and well-being. On the international level, the United Nations finally raised the issue of Indigenous rights in the 1990s, and in 2000 they established the United Nations Permanent Forum on Indigenous Issues.

Nevertheless, despite these events, Natives everywhere still face considerable challenges. In the United States today, there are 2.9 million Natives, or 0.9 percent of the population, and 5.2 million Natives mixed with other races, or 1.7 percent of the population.[12] At 11 percent, our unemployment rate is almost double the national rate of 6.2 percent, while our median incomes are a third lower than the national average.[13] Our high school drop-out rates are nearly twice as high as the national average,[14] while our youth are three and a half times more likely to commit suicide.[15] According to U.S. Department of Justice records, one in three Native American women are raped in their lifetimes, a figure that is two and a half times greater than the average for all U.S. women. In 86 percent of cases of rape of Indigenous women and girls, the rapist is non-Native, which results in many crimes going uninvestigated by either U.S. or tribal officials, because the jurisdiction is unclear.[16] While Native American youth only make up 1.8 percent of the total youth population, they represent 3.6 percent of those detained, and once they are in the prison system, they are more likely to be placed in detention and less likely to get probation.[17]

Natives face special health challenges and disparities too, from having the highest rates of diabetes, heart disease, and asthma among any racial/ethnic group, to experiencing persistent barriers to health care and insurance. Tuberculosis, mental illness, major cardiovascular diseases, pneumonia, cancer, infant mortality, and

maternal complications are other issues that disproportionately impact Natives.[18]

Urban Indians—those of us who live somewhere
other than on reservations—face unique challenges.
Federal funding does not always directly address our
needs, and the safety net available to Natives living on
reservations or tribal territories is unavailable to most
of us. The magnitude of this problem is significant, as
urban Indians make up more than 70 percent of the
Native population overall.[19]

So, although Native American people who are alive
today are proud, strong survivors against all odds, we
continue to face some of the most dire socioeconomic
conditions of any group in America. There is no question that the complicated set of issues facing us today are
rooted in hundreds of years of colonization, suffering,
and trauma.

Trauma

If you have personally experienced a traumatic event
such as a great loss, or a violation or abuse, you know
how it destroys your trust, your sense of safety, even your
sense of who you are. In order to survive trauma, you
react unconsciously to protect yourself, usually using an
automatic survival strategy like dissociation, fight, flight,
or appeasing. Often these self-protection and defense
mechanisms stick with you, coloring your perception
from then on of everyone you meet and everything that
happens, especially if you are traumatized more than
once. After a while, you have less and less choice in the
matter; the protective stance hardens into a way of seeing
and experiencing the world. It feels like the way you are:
I'm just distant. I'm just unemotional. I'm just suspicious.

I'm just small and unthreatening. I'm just mean and aggressive. You have blinders on about what is possible for yourself and for human interactions, and you don't even know how much they limit the possibilities.

Unfortunately, almost every one of us alive on earth has experienced some kind of trauma. So chances are you know what I am talking about. But now imagine if you came from generations of people who were systematically and repeatedly violated in every possible way. Imagine that all your family and friends and community members regularly experienced traumatic events: upheaval, violence, rape, brainwashing, homelessness, forced marches, criminalization, denigration, and murder, over hundreds of years. Imagine the trauma of this experience has been reinforced by government policies, economic systems, and social norms that have systematically denied your people access to safety, mobility, resources, food, education, dignity, and positive reflections of themselves. Repeated and ongoing violation, exploitation, and deprivation have a deep, lasting traumatic impact, not just at the individual level but on whole populations, tribes, and nations. This is what's known as collective trauma, historic trauma, intergenerational trauma.

The relatively new field of epigenetics studies how trauma that our ancestors experienced can literally be passed down, attached to our DNA. An essay in a 2013 issue of *Discover* magazine described it:

> Like silt deposited on the cogs of a finely tuned machine after the seawater of a tsunami recedes, our experiences, and those of our forebears, are never gone, even if they have been forgotten. They become a part of us, a molecular residue holding fast to our genetic scaffolding.[20]

It was found, for example, that the descendants of Holocaust survivors were found to have different cortisone profiles than normal, which was an adaptation to prolonged starvation, since cortisol impacts the ability of certain organs to use glucose and metabolic fuels.

My central metaphor for the subject of colonization is the body, because we each instinctively understand our body's sense of sovereignty and the sense of violation. The initial phase of colonization—the conquest—is like a rape, causing the first wave of trauma. Later—when the colonizers set down roots and become settlers—colonization becomes more like a virus that every human institution and system as well as every human being carries inside. The collective body—the nation and culture of settlers and surviving colonized people—adapts, passing down these adaptations in their genes over generations. Yet the adaptations don't constitute healing. The virus remains: the original seeds of separation—fear of the Other—that lead to ongoing acts of control and exploitation.

The colonizer virus inside culture and institutions is especially dangerous. Our education system reflects the colonizer virus. So does our agriculture and food system. So does our foreign policy. So does our environmental policy. So does the field of design. And so do the realms of wealth, the subject of this book: investment, finance, and philanthropy.

Decolonization

Decolonization, obviously, is the process of undoing colonization. The Afro-Caribbean philosopher and revolutionary Frantz Fanon described decolonization using a famous line from the Bible: "The last shall be first and the first last."[21] Taken literally, decolonization means that the land that was stolen is returned, and sovereignty over not only the land and its resources but also over social structures and traditions is granted back to those from whom it was all stolen.

Yet decolonization defined like this tends to get stuck and make no headway at all. The truth is there is no future that does not include the settlers occupying Indigenous lands. Today, in the twenty-first century, Indigenous and settler lives, families, and businesses are intertwined. This is simply the pragmatic reality of today's world. What we *can* focus on with decolonization is stopping the cycles of abuse and healing ourselves from trauma. In this way we expand our possibilities for the future.

We must heal ourselves by each taking responsibility for our part in creating or maintaining the colonial virus. We must identify and reject the colonized aspects of our culture and our institutions so that we can heal. In healing we eradicate the colonizer virus from society: instead of *divide, control, exploit,* we embrace a new paradigm of *connect, relate, belong.*

<u>COLONIZED → DECOLONIZED</u>

DIVIDE → CONNECT

CONTROL → RELATE

EXPLOIT → BELONG

There are already people working on decolonizing projects in many sectors. There's a decolonized cookbook. There is decolonized curriculum being developed for schools. *Teen Vogue* ran a story in February 2018, "Indigenous Land Acknowledgement, Explained."[22] There's a game called Cards Against Colonization, a play on Cards Against Humanity. A doctor in San Francisco is partnering with Native health care providers to define what decolonized health care looks like. She is already teaching it to medical students. Two researchers out of Stanford are investigating how the colonial mentality influenced organizational design and are proposing tools for decolonizing organizational processes.

My contribution is to address the sectors of banking, investment, finance, philanthropy, and all their institutions and processes. They—we—are all deeply infected with the colonizer virus. Wealth is used to divide us and control us and exploit us, but it doesn't have to be.

CHAPTER TWO

Arriving at the Plantation

How the design, architecture, and location
of financial institutions reflect and maintain
colonization

In 2005, I was finishing my masters in health care administration at the University of North Carolina at Chapel Hill. Most of my friends in the program were going into hospital administration—it's what our degree was focused on, and there's big money to make in running hospitals. I had interviewed at a few of them, like the Mayo Clinic, but I just didn't feel right about it. All they really wanted to know was if I could figure out how to save them money: healing and helping people was not the first order of business at all. I interviewed at the consulting firm Deloitte too. None of these jobs felt like ministry, like medicine, like truly being of service. My professor told me there was an opportunity at a foundation, the Kate B. Reynolds Charitable Trust (KBR), and that they were interested in talking to me.

"I think you should go," he said.

Frankly, that didn't sound appealing either. For starters, I was not interested in living in Winston-Salem. It might be North Carolina's fourth-largest city, but that isn't saying much. I had my sights set on a *real* city, which at the time meant DC or Atlanta for this country boy. Still, I dutifully drove to the foundation for my first interview. My old Honda Civic rolled onto the idyllic property—acres of manicured lawns and gardens, a main house with 22 windows flanking the front, a chapel, and a greenhouse. The property even had a name, Reynolda. I had never been to a house with a name. What kind of person names his house?

Reynolda was built by R. J. Reynolds, the tobacco tycoon. When I picture R. J., I think of the Great Gatsby as played by Leonardo DiCaprio: charming and gregarious but also entitled and clueless. R. J.'s father had been a large-scale land and slave owner, a merchant, and a tobacco farmer. By 1860, when R. J. was 10 years old, his father owned two dozen properties, more than 10,000 acres. His 59 slaves made him one of the largest slaveholders in Virginia. After the Civil War, R. J. and his siblings had to help their father adapt to a world without slave labor. African Americans—now freedmen—were still critical to the tobacco business—now as sharecroppers and tenant farmers.

In 1874, R. J. sold his shares in the family business and started his own tobacco company in Winston with his younger brother William Neal. Things really took off for them after they invented prepackaged cigarettes. Long the county's most eligible bachelor, R. J. finally settled down, got hitched, and built the 1,000-plus acre estate, Reynolda, basically a self-contained village for Reynolds employees and their families.

During his lifetime, R. J. supported many charities: schools, churches, orphanages, and hospitals. When he passed away in 1917, he was the wealthiest person in the state by a wide margin. His wife and his children continued his philanthropy, forming several foundations with the family money. The Reynolds name is on buildings everywhere in these parts. Kate B., for whom the Kate B. Reynolds Charitable Trust is named, was the wife of R. J.'s younger brother and business partner William Neal Reynolds.[1]

In other words, this was quintessential "old money," the inherited wealth of established upper-class families, sometimes called "gentry," or the "de facto aristocracy" because the United States isn't supposed to have an actual aristocratic class. On top of the colonial culture that goes with old money, the Trust also reflected the culture of banking.

In 1947, the Trust was created with just under $5 million from Mrs. Reynolds's estate put in trust at Wachovia Bank, her personal bank. By 1988, assets totaled $129 million. A year later, a New York investment banking firm successfully completed a leveraged buyout of RJR Nabisco, including R. J. Reynolds Tobacco Company, and the Trust received $100 per share of its 2.4 million shares. Literally overnight, Trust assets doubled (several folks in Winston-Salem became instant millionaires), and the Trust began to review opportunities to reduce its initial tax liability by channeling some of the gain to qualified charitable organizations. They also decided to move the staffing structure outside the bank given the drastic increase in assets. Since then, from its more than 2 million shares of R. J. Reynolds Co. stock, the Trust has grown to over $530 million in assets and uses three-fourths of the investment income collected each year to improve the health of low-income people across the state, and the other fourth "to help the poor and needy" in Winston-Salem.

The irony that wealth made from cigarettes is being used to improve health is mostly lost on the community, eager to get a piece of the pie.

Because KBR was literally born and operated from a bank, banking culture prevailed. For most of its history, the leadership of the foundation had been drawn from within Wachovia or employees who left the bank to run the external operations. The first president was at Wachovia for 28 years before joining the foundation. He started out in the traditional role of a bank trust officer. He joined the foundation two years after the buyout of RJR Nabisco. He maintained a relatively formal, impersonal culture, including strict business attire. Men wore white dress shirts, neckties, and wingtip shoes. The foundation office—specifically built to resemble the original buildings on the Reynolda property, I later learned—had white walls, and all the furniture was heavy, wooden, and antique. It felt like a different time period inside the office.

It was my first experience of how anachronistic the field of philanthropy is, how formal, how distanced from ordinary people's lives and experiences. The atmosphere that compels you to lower your voice and speak in a whisper when you enter. The lack of warmth and personality, the uncomfortable seating, the priceless antiques you're petrified of breaking. Obviously all this is true of most bank buildings too, not to mention investment firms: all the hard edges, polished marble and glass and metal surfaces, the divided, soundproofed offices, the mostly rectangular meeting tables.

This observation turned out to be a recurring theme in my conversations with other people of color working as funders. One colleague, an Asian American, took a job with a corporate foundation after being recruited at the age of 27. Her portfolio alone was six to eight million dollars, with the whole place dispersing $30 million a year. She remembers her first day:

> I was wearing a business suit and really nice shoes, because the place was formal, business attire, very professional. I walked in and it's on the 13th floor, overlooking the water and the bridge. A view as beautiful as the day. I had a computer and my own office. And I was just like, "Holy crap. Have I arrived?" It was so quiet. And sterile. Not a lot of color, lots of gray. I just went in quietly and sat down in my office. My glass-walled office. I was used to working in basements and vans, around trash bags and vomit. It didn't compute.
>
> Of course, I was also kind of digging it, my own office where I could close my door and make my phone calls. It felt very special and also very scary. I didn't want to mess things up.[2]

A Latina colleague remembers her first impressions of the institution that hired her:

> It's set on a campus. There are deer hopping around. There was something about the place that makes you feel like you're entering a mausoleum. You almost want to whisper. I was like, "What is it about this that bothers me so much?" I couldn't place it for a long time. I think it's about wanting to silence reality to some extent. There is something powerful about the choice to physically remove yourself from the reality of the

issues that you are working on. I couldn't name it at the moment, but it has stayed with me for a long, long time.[3]

You know there's a style of architecture called "colonial," right? It's not even one style, it encompasses all the examples of a colonizer's style of building and the materials used in building in the home country, transplanted to the colony, so there are French colonial houses, Dutch colonial, and Spanish colonial. Embarrassingly for Britain, if there's no country named, a plain old colonial building can be assumed to refer to British style.

There's no doubt: most of institutions that move and control money exhibit colonial style. This is how the separation paradigm I mentioned in Chapter 1 shows up in design and architecture.

Professional buildings intentionally feel different from spaces where people live. The cold, hard style and feel of these spaces allows the decisions made there to be impersonal and rigid, following rules rather than flexibly adapting to the complexity of human situations. Their location, architecture, and design support colonizing tactics of division, control, and exploitation, which is why I call these spaces "ivory towers."

Colonial Social Architecture

Just as the architects who were behind the physical space made design choices to reinforce the Us vs. Them separation worldview, there were also architects of the *organizational design* who made choices that had serious consequences.

Organizational design determines fundamental elements like how power is held and by whom, who makes decisions and how decisions are carried out, what the relationship of the organization is to resources, and what constitutes success, effectiveness, purpose, etc.

Most organizations and institutions operating in the world today, and particularly those that handle money, reflect the design principles of the social architects of the industrial revolution and the scientific revolution. They were mostly philosophers, economists, scientists, and statesmen working in the late 1700s through the early 1900s: almost exclusively white men who privileged the rational (the mind) over all else, intoxicated with the separation paradigm. When the philanthropic and social sector were developed in the early part of the twentieth century, the design elements were the same: bureaucracy, competition, specialization, and consolidation of power and resources. Tradition and the status quo were worshipped, resulting in conformity, formality, and arrogance. In other words, separation, separation, and more separation.

"It's not hard to map the neocolonial DNA across our sector . . . the effect of concentrating power, hyperprofessionalizing in a way that creates exclusivity, co-opting existing culture, forcing assimilation, leveraging local populations to obtain resources, and reinforcing larger systems of oppression," write Stanford scholars Jess Rimington and Joanna Levitt Cea, who are cataloging the hallmarks of "colonized organizational design" in both the nonprofit and for-profit sectors.[4]

The social architects developed a strict hierarchy of authority, the pyramid model, in which the small number of the Us perched at the very top, holding the authority and the vision. Pyramid processes are top-down, closed-door, and expert-driven. Populating the base of the pyramid, with the greatest numbers but the least power, were the Them—the Others, basically—less human and less valuable, due to receive fewer rights and resources. In between were middlemen (only more recently also middlewomen) who implemented the vision of the top and kept the bottom aligned to that vision.

Once these kinds of organizational structures became the norm, resources could be effectively extracted and consolidated for those at the top. The extracted and consolidated wealth was guarded and preserved for the Us, and kept away from the Them, which further reinforced the division between Haves and Have Nots. A particular type of ownership model grew dominant: the publicly traded corporation, in which shares of ownership are traded in the stock market among the elite. The extent of the wealth was often hidden, especially from those at the bottom of the pyramid. The fundamental dynamic is a one-way flow of resources—whether that means money, services, or information—from those more fortunate (the Haves) to the less fortunate (Have Nots).

In these organizations, the experience of the least empowered people/roles—often relegated to less intellectual, more physical tasks—is that their time has less value and is therefore compensated with less pay. Their thoughts are also less valued, their voices discouraged. Their experience of work feels more anonymous, more interchangeable, less meaningful, than the experience at the top of the pyramid. Their individuality and personal creative expression is likely not welcome in, and possibly strictly prohibited from, the workplace.

Leadership as designed by these same architects reflected the "great man theory," where the leader is basically the alpha male. Usually white and heterosexual, and compared with the other straight white men, he is the strongest, most educated, and most focused, ruthless and relentless in pursuing goals. He knows where to go, what to do, how to do it, and his followers understand their role simply as: follow his lead. This leadership style is rigid and transactional. The leader's commands must be followed, otherwise the consequences are discipline and punishment, so it's often called "command-and-control leadership."

In their *Dismantling Racism* workbook, Kenneth Jones and Tema Okun identified other characteristics of white supremacy culture, including perfectionism, sense of urgency, defensiveness, quantity over quality, worship of the written word, paternalism, either/or thinking, fear of open conflict, individualism, worship of unlimited growth, objectivity, and avoidance of discomfort. They note that these "are used as norms and standards without being pro-actively named or chosen.... Organizations which unconsciously use these characteristics as their norms and standards make it difficult, if not impossible, to open the door to other cultural norms and standards. As a result, many of our organizations, while saying we want to be multicultural, really only allow other people and cultures to come in if they adapt or conform to already existing cultural norms."[5]

Colonial, white supremacist organizational practices seem inevitable because they were so universally adopted over the next centuries, and they still govern the great majority of our institutions, but they were *design choices*. This means that other choices are available, even when they seem far-fetched. We know what spaces and organizations look like, feel like, and function like when they are inspired by the colonizers' principles of separation, competition, and exploitation. How would they be different if they were based on principles like integration and interdependence, reciprocity and relationship?

CHAPTER THREE

House Slaves

How diversity efforts backfire and reinforce
colonization

The president of the Kate B. Reynolds Charitable Trust was new. Never before in its history had the foundation chosen a woman to be president. She compelled me to come back for a second interview, and then a third. By the third, I was coming to terms with the job: *You're telling me that if I came to work here as a "program officer," I would basically be giving away 25 million dollars a year to whoever I think should get it. So what's the catch?*

After confirming that I had no "skeletons hidden in my closet" and that I was just an honest-to-goodness Southern Christian boy, I was offered the job. I also had to agree to a code of conduct that included no public drunkenness or swearing, among other things.

I said yes, making me her first hire. Me, this little brown kid, just 28 years old, and usually taken for even younger. (I've got a small frame, and back then I was a 28 waist too. Those were the days.)

Why did I take the job? I trusted my gut. Something within my heart told me that this was a good place for me to do God's work.

Also, the money. I signed on for $65,000, making me the highest paid person in my graduating class; the residency programs in hospital management typically paid $40,000. It wasn't long before my salary was bumped up further, and only a couple of years before I was making six figures. For the first time in my life I felt financially secure. My salary was unimaginable for someone in my family. Not to mention the perks. The paid holidays! We'd have a very fancy holiday party around December 10, and then we were off until January 6 or 8. We just shut down the office, and got paid for it. Lots of vacation time. On top of the pay, we got a 10 percent bonus every paycheck, instead of having a retirement fund, because we had so few employees.

After one year there, I bought a beautiful brand new house, because I'd listened to Oprah growing up, and she had driven home the message that home ownership was the anchor of wealth. I had subscribed to the American Dream.

When the foundation suggested that I get rid of my old Honda Civic because it didn't represent their image (the legacy of wealth), I went to the dealership to look at a nicer used car, but they had something less modest in mind for me: *oh no, you work at Kate B. Reynolds. You guys do such good work in the community.* They gave me an incredible deal on a brand new Volvo S60, right out of the showroom. It was outside my budget, but they made it work. Now I was really living the dream.

That brings me to the other reason the job was irresistible: the prestige. I received automatic respect from the community. I knew the mayor of the town. My first Christmas I received hundreds of Christmas cards, including one from the governor of the state, a real card that she actually signed. I'd roll up in my foundation-sponsored car (they provided a car for business trips so I got saved from putting miles on my new Volvo) at the hospital for a site visit in Southern Pines, a very wealthy neighborhood, and the CEO always met me at the front door. I couldn't help but think, *Wow, I am Somebody now.*

Everywhere I went I was catered to, even to an embarrassing degree. One time I casually mentioned that I liked to drink diet Dr. Pepper. All of a sudden, our refrigerator in the office was stocked with diet Dr. Pepper, although I was the only one in the office who drank it. Then I noticed when I went out into the community for meetings it was always available. *Why is there diet Dr. Pepper everywhere? Is this the most popular drink now or what?* I asked someone, "Do you all drink diet Dr. Pepper?" No, they had called my office and asked what I liked to drink. It was almost too much.

For the first time in my life I could demand things of people, and I'd have my way. When my family needed medical care, I called ahead. *Momma, you give them my name.* And for the first time in her life she got first-class service everywhere. I can't say I wasn't proud.

~~~

A lot of people of color go into philanthropy and social finance for the same reasons I did. For many of us, it's about purpose: we earnestly hope, and sometimes believe, that we can connect the foundation's assets with our drive to improve outcomes for the planet and its people, especially people in our own communities.

"I get a role in deploying resources in a way that creates equity in communities that need more equitable outcomes. Even though I'm not white, working in philanthropy can give me some access to that white privilege," one colleague told me.[1]

Another colleague of mine said, "I value community. I value close relationships with people. I value a strong sense of purpose, feeling like I'm making a difference."[2] A Black man from the South shared that he was recruited into philanthropy after—and because—he'd spent a long time doing work in the very community that the foundation wanted to fund.

> I wasn't chasing a gig in philanthropy, that's for damn sure. I had worked on the other side for a decade and had interacted with foundations and donors throughout that entire time. With foundations it was usually challenging. I felt like I was often talking to people who . . . I don't know how to say it except that they were lost in their ego. It was because they were moving money, but it was money that wasn't theirs. They had no clue as to what was going on in my community, what we were really trying to accomplish, which further exaggerated the already weird power dynamic. There was no mutual respect in the relationship.

> But the person who recruited me was an exception, someone I did trust in philanthropy, who had been a good partner to me. As my program officer she not only funded me, she kept in contact with me beyond the requirements of the grant. She created less distance between herself and her grantee partners than most foundation program staff would do. Her foundation thought it would be helpful to have someone who was from the South, who was Black, who knew

racial justice work in the South to come run a portfolio that was designed to address racial justice issues in the South. So I said yes. Once I went over to the foundation side and became a peer as opposed to a grantee, my relationships with people in philanthropy completely changed. Everyone was nicer. They wanted to support my leadership.[3]

Many of us come into the work after doing public service or community organizing like he had done, having experienced philanthropy from the "other side of the table," when we were seeking funding. Most of this grassroots work in our communities is compensated very poorly, and sometimes even on a volunteer basis. So if we're honest about it, the pay and the prestige are also very compelling.

One colleague was recruited by a foundation when she was just 27. She and her family were refugees from Vietnam, and she learned English as her second language when they settled in Texas. The job offer came during a recession.

I was poor, I was young. They were offering me $40,000 to $50,000, basically $30,000 more than I was making. I needed literally to make rent, I had no assets, maybe $400 in my checking account. And I was hungry to be in a place where I had a tiny bit more authority than where I had been before.[4]

"The only reason I entertained the offer is because they pay, and nobody else paid," as another Black colleague of mine put it.[5]

Tokens and Model Minorities

So that's why I took the job, why we all took the jobs. But why were we hired?

It should go without saying that I was qualified for the job. I came from a great university program—the University of North Carolina at Chapel Hill was among the best. And it was just over an hour away, so the university and the foundation knew people in common who knew and vouched for me. Also, I had valuable, relevant experience—while completing my studies I'd been working for seven years with a national nonprofit organization that did health advocacy work.

On top of that, the new president was deliberate about wanting to diversify the staff in terms of age and race/ethnicity. Ah, diversity. It's one of those words that's been stretched and diluted until it's come to mean too much and then, not much of anything at all. "Diversity" is how white people talk about race when they don't want to talk about race, but it also can mean the representation of any marginalized group, including Indigenous people, women, queer folk, people with disabilities, immigrants, and people of particular religious or ethnic backgrounds. It can mean people with different mindsets and values, or people of different ages and people from different parts of the country.

For the foundation, I checked a lot of boxes, being a Native American—often taken for Latino—but a Native who dresses, speaks, and behaves in a mainstream way. And in terms of increasing age diversity, I sure was young, relative to the field. I was the youngest program officer in North Carolina—and I was among the youngest in the country.

Foundations and financial institutions let a few token people of color in, because they see that we have a different quality of access to our communities and because we have some type of wisdom that they want, but we're expected to completely assimilate. Imagine you married into a very wealthy family that is all about keeping up appearances. You are expected to conform to their behavior and their way of acting and interacting and moving through the world. That's what it's like. They will view you the way Rose's mother (played by Frances Fisher) stared at Jack (played by Leonardo DiCaprio) in the movie *Titanic*. She "looked at him like an insect. A dangerous insect which must be squashed quickly." (Yes, I saw the movie 12 times in 1998.) If you contradict them, you will be reviled or silenced. If you bring your full self to work, they will push you out. If you reveal any of the craziness or dark secrets that run in the family, they will excommunicate you.

Tokens end up on tiptoe, always on our best behavior. This is heightened by the sense that we still often have the feeling that we are representing our entire race, that everything we do will reflect on all other Latinos or Blacks or Asian Americans or Natives. Who's going to speak truth to power when there could be negative consequences for everyone who looks like you, not just in this moment but into the foreseeable future?

A Black colleague from the South admitted:

> By my fourth day, I had already begun to regret taking the job. . . . The truth is, I've never felt quite like I could bring my full self to the job. I never felt like I could speak freely. I feel like I have to play a role. I myself have become more conservative in how I operate. Not in my

thinking, but how I move through the world. It's almost like an expectation that you yourself get in line. Not even an expectation—it's required. You have to assimilate in order to be able to move anything inside of a foundation. You have to drink the Kool-Aid and operate like they do, move like they do.[6]

"I feel hyper self-consciousness when I enter very white spaces," a Latina colleague says. "I am very aware of my hands moving, my accent. I am very aware of it. Even if I am proud of it, I'm still very aware of it."[7] Another colleague told me, "I was scared shitless because I had just left an organization where I 'played the race card too early' and had shot myself in the foot as a result. So I basically kept my head down hard working for about a year before I did anything that revealed anything about me personally. Looking back, I was trying to build unassailable credibility and just be really, really good at the work."[8] Yet another colleague says, "I'm always trying to play that game of chess of what are they expecting from me as an Asian American woman, as somebody who's kind of mid-level professional, and where do I push some of the assumptions versus where do I not rock the boat because I just make things harder for myself?"[9]

According to authors Rebecca Stone and Benjamin Butler, in *Core Issues in Comprehensive Community-Building Initiatives: Exploring Power and Race and in Structural Racism and Community Building*: "Foundations may unwittingly perpetuate a dominant worldview, one that is highly racialized and often dictated by white European culture. In an organizational environment governed by the dominant worldview, individuals are prone to making decisions from an ethnocentric vantage point."[10]

A common way the leadership in philanthropy conveys its doubt in our ability and credibility is to bring in independent consultants to research the very issues that we have intimate knowledge of from our time living in and/or working with communities on the ground. It was this very expertise for which we were often hired. As expressed by a Black colleague from the South:

> We had to hire a consulting firm the last six months to do a full scan of [the field], just to bring it back to my boss and to his boss to say everything that I've been saying for the last year. Literally the report is verbatim all of the stuff that I had brought up, but no one heard it, or it wasn't given the same weight without having some sort of outside external person who was paid a lot of money to say it and put it nice and neatly down on paper. That's the game that we're forced to play.[11]

His experience was echoed by an investigation commissioned by the Association of Black Foundation Executives (ABFE) that looked into a concerning trend: the inability of the philanthropic sector to hold on to Black employees. ABFE's investigation culminated in a 2014 report called "The Exit Interview," which found that many Black professionals left because they felt extra scrutinized and their expertise was not trusted.[12]

An Asian American colleague talks about the frequent assumption or intimation that the (only) grantmaker of color from a given community has an unprofessional personal agenda. She's been called "righteous" ("and not in a good way," she quips) for defending her recommendation to fund people-of-color-led organizations. It's a double-edged sword, she says: "When it's convenient for a foundation, they'll parade around the diversity and say, 'Look, we reflect the wider community.' But then our conundrum becomes how do we advocate for our community without being accused of becoming too passionate, of playing favorites."[13]

I also felt I had to do acrobatics around staying "objective and professional," not seeming to favor Native American grantseekers. Of course, this is exactly what championing equity involves, so it's a ridiculous and strenuous expectation. I had to do a lot of extra explaining to give myself credibility, especially to our all-white board and to the good old boys network among our grantees, who at first seemed incredulous that a boyish brown man was holding the key to their treasure box.

When, upon getting a job in an ivory tower, you are made to feel like you won the lottery, part of what is communicated to you is that there are many, many others ready to take your place. You're replaceable. And there are only so many "designated minority" positions to go around. That position can easily be reallocated to another "poor and needy" candidate to keep the quota filled. It's a subtle way to keep you behaving well, assimilating to the culture, working like a dog. Whether or not it is deliberate, as the only one of our kind, we often hear how lucky we are to work in this esteemed and powerful field. *Boy, you were given the chance of a lifetime!*

Now, there is no doubt it is a privilege to work in a field that controls and moves money, whether it's banking or investing or philanthropy. It is. I don't want to take away that it is. I just want to say that I feel like it's a privilege for these fields to have me, too.

Foundations often seek out young "model minorities" like me who are the first to "make it" in our families. Yet here's the thing about institutions—or any systems, really—that were created by and for a certain kind of person (white straight men, say) that then decide they want to "be inclusive" or "open their doors to diversity" or "commit to equity"—having a seat at the table is not the same as feeling free to speak in your own voice, to offer your own divergent ideas, to bring your full self to bear on the work.

~~~

To be clear, most of us are still "token" Others in an almost pure-white world. The statistics are dismal regarding the number of white men vs. Others inside the ivory tower institutions controlling wealth. Three-fourths of foundations' full-time staff are white.[14] According to the D5 Coalition's 2016 report *State of the Work*, fewer than a third of program officers (32.3 percent) and about 8 percent of foundation CEOs are people of color.[15] Only 3 percent of philanthropic institutions are led by Black chief executives, with even more dismal representation for other races and ethnicities.[16]

Board leadership is even more demographically starved. "Fully 85 percent of foundation board members are white, while just 7 percent are African American and only 4 percent are Hispanic," says Gara LaMarche, the president of the Democracy Alliance. "Nearly three-quarters of foundations have no written policy on board diversity."[17] Since joining the board of the Andrus Family Fund in 2017, I am one of only two Native Americans on a national private foundation board.

Along the rest of the loans-to-gifts spectrum, the management of financial services is 81 percent white. African Americans account for just 2.7 percent of senior-level staff.[18] When it comes to venture capital, the disparities are even starker: VCs are overwhelmingly white (88 percent) and male. Just 1 percent are Black—not really a surprise, when only four of the Fortune 500 companies have Black CEOs—and less than 1 percent are Latino. No one even mentions the numbers for Native Americans.[19] Minority angel investors make up just 3.6 percent of total angel investors.[20]

And then there's humanitarian aid. In a 2008 article called "The New Colonialists" in *Foreign Policy,* the authors critique the "hodgepodge of international charities, aid agencies, philanthropists, and foreign advisers" who "are increasingly taking over key state functions, providing for the health, welfare, and safety of citizens" in many so-called developing nations. They continue:

> In much the same way European empires once dictated policies across their colonial holdings, the new colonialists—among them international development groups such as Oxfam, humanitarian nongovernmental organizations (NGOs) like Doctors Without Borders and Mercy Corps, and mega-philanthropies like the Bill & Melinda Gates Foundation—direct development strategies and craft government policies for their hosts. But though the new colonialists are the glue holding society together in many weak states, their presence often deepens the dependency of these states on outsiders.[21]

"There's certainly a thought that if you have a more diverse workforce and if you have a more diverse group of suppliers, that institutions very well could do a better job of understanding a more diverse marketplace and how to best serve it," *Mother Jones* quoted the head of the diversity office at the Consumer Financial Protection Bureau as saying.[22] Yes, and while the numbers should be cause for alarm, a focus on just balancing out the numbers is not enough. Diversity statistics that get held up as a sole measure of progress are an insufficient measure, because we need to go beyond mere representation, to access to power and ownership.

#diversityfails

In philanthropy there have been dozens of initiatives on diversity, equity, and inclusion, often lumped together using the acronym DEI. The field has spent hundreds of thousands, maybe millions, on making these buzzwords the subject of conference topics, task forces, summits, surveys, reports, and trainings. Vu Le, a nonprofit leader who frequently writes and speaks about the sector, using humor to point out a lot of our stuck places and particular afflictions, describes the hot air:

> When we just talk about Equity and go no further, we are guilty of Fakequity. . . . People seem to think that forming an equity committee, talking about equity, sending staff and board to trainings, "listening" to communities, conducting research and gathering data, and adding terminologies to websites and brochures are sufficient to achieving equity. But no, these things are necessary, but not sufficient.[23]

A Latina colleague summed it up: "I always want to stab myself in the eye with a pencil because it is the same old conversation."[24]

One of the colleagues I interviewed was asked to form what ultimately wound up being named the DICE committee: "We couldn't decide on the title. Some people wanted diversity. Some wanted inclusion, others equity. Some wanted cultural humility, so we decided to throw it all in the pot because I got tired of meeting after meeting just devoted to naming ourselves instead of doing the work."[25]

Another colleague recalls a diversity initiative that was launched at her workplace. The organizers led her and her colleagues through the exercise commonly called the "Privilege Walk," where everyone starts in one line in the middle of the room, and you step forward or step back based on what kind of barriers or privileges you encountered in life. For example, "Take a step back if anyone in your family's ever been incarcerated. . . . Step forward if you grew up with more than five books in the house. . . . Step back if you've ever been a victim of violence," and so on.

> An African American guy, a friend of mine, and I, we started stepping back. And with every question we kept stepping back. It only took eight questions for us to hit the back wall. And they kept asking questions and we couldn't step back any further. It was like the pit of inequality. It was so deep that we just sat down. There wasn't enough space in the room to physically show how many barriers we had overcome to get to where we were. Everyone else was towards the middle or the very front of the room. Some people were so far in front that they couldn't go forward any further. It was a big room, but not big enough for their privilege.
>
> It brought up all kinds of feelings. Was I just a pity-party?

Would all of us in that room who had to keep working together just pretend like we hadn't seen how different our lives had been to get to this same place?

What is the toll of being public and proud about how long the road has been, about your determination and resilience and grit?

What's the emotional and psychological toll it takes to educate others about what privilege means?

How far can resilience stretch when there's continuous re-traumatization—at what point do the psyche and the soul just shatter?[26]

It is undeniably difficult for people of color to be successful in the ivory tower institutions of wealth. The few of us who have pushed through and stayed for more than a decade have learned to coach each other through all the racism, the weirdness, the guilt, the uncomfortable power dynamics. Possibly we were fortunate enough to land in an environment where we could be a little bit more authentic to who we are.

What we know is that talk—meaning everything from conducting research to holding sensitivity trainings to writing formal policies—is not enough, whether it's talk about diversity, equity, or inclusion. Sometimes all the talk is outright counterproductive. Studies show that it can activate bias, create resentment, or spark a backlash (or a "whitelash"). In fact, despite all of the dollars and hours invested in efforts inside philanthropy, the newest data from the Council on Foundations shows that the number of people of color and the number of women in philanthropy has actually decreased.[27] Studies also show that efforts to support diversity in corporate settings are often counterproductive, because the approach follows more of the same divisive, dominating colonial tactics. "Your organization will become less diverse, not more, if you require managers to go to diversity training, try to regulate their hiring and promotion decisions, and put in a legalistic grievance system," wrote Frank Dobbin and Alexandra Kalev in the *Harvard Business Review* in 2016, calling this the "classic command-and-control approach to diversity."[28]

Diversity talk allows people to deny racism. It lets white folks ignore persistent, alarming racial inequalities and discriminatory policies and practices. It lets people off the hook about their responsibility in maintaining a colonial white supremacist society. Andrea Armeni, the executive director of Transform Finance, calls "diversity and inclusion" initiatives "false solutions" to inequity and injustice:

> Having some managers of color is definitely a step in the right direction, and a very much needed one. But that doesn't, per se, bring us anywhere towards racial justice. Looking at how many people of color are on the board or in top management of a corporation doesn't really tell me about whether, at large, communities of color are benefiting. You could have Halliburton run by African Americans; it's still not necessarily a racially just organization.[29]

~~~

A good question is: Why *should* ivory towers hire people like me?

Those most excluded and exploited by today's broken economy possess exactly the perspective and wisdom needed to fix it. Ironically, the separation paradigm that locked us out and made us Others actually cultivated our resilience strategies. To survive the trauma of exploitation, we always had to believe that the dominant worldview was only one option, even when it seemed ubiquitous and inevitable. This has made us masters of alternative possibilities.

In their intoxicated rush to consolidate wealth, colonizers reduced the number of religions, languages, species, cultures, social systems, media channels, and political systems. On all scales, global to local, this homogenizing campaign—*global bleaching*, you could call it—made the world not just more bland and boring, but also less innovative and less resilient. Evolution and innovation arise from difference and variation, not from sameness. These are fundamental principles of life. For us to have carried inside ourselves the possibility or even hope of a different world is powerful all by itself.

More concretely speaking, we who are Others translate effectively between the world of the funder and the world of those seeking funding, because we ourselves have to switch between worlds all the time. "Codeswitching" is the term linguists adopted to describe switching between more than one language in a conversation, but it also has come to mean the shift between cultures as revealed in word choice, accents, and styles of expression. A classic example is the Southerner who hides his accent when he goes to work in a Manhattan law firm. It's particularly common among people of color and colonized people.

Over our lifetimes nonwhite people learn to smoothly transition between the language of the powerful—standard "white" English—and our cultural dialects. We constantly make split-second choices about our cadences and inflections and expressions, based on with whom we are talking. We hold back our most authentic expressions of our self, whether in language, clothing, or the stories we share, waiting first to see if it feels safe to do so. We become expert navigators of difference, cultivating this level of awareness in a way our white colleagues, especially the monolingual ones, never have to. It's a burden, but it's also a superpower, as it turns out.

Chris Cardona, a colleague at the Ford Foundation whose parents were immigrants from Colombia, grew up around his *abuelitos* in Colombia and, later, with godparents in Massachusetts whom he called Grandma and Grandpa. "Bridging is something I think that many Latinos have," he says. "Language shapes the way that we understand and interact with the world, and having access to more than one language provides a broader set of perspectives: You can see different realities and connect them."[30]

Working with people who are different from you, in a culture that is not your own, using language that is not the way you naturally express yourself—these challenges push your brain to expand its habitual ways of thinking and sharpen its performance. "Boundary spanning" is another way of describing this capacity, and it's often considered a specialty of those of us outside the dominant culture. This also tends to make us particularly skilled at coalition building, specifically the ability to come together around common ground despite differing identities. We often possess the ability to hold multiple realities simultaneously: our thinking unifies, contains, and transcends oppositions, a stance that's really needed in the current divided and divisive sociocultural-political climate.

Talking about the entrepreneurs of color who get just 1 percent of funding, consultant Ryan Bowers commented, "They're usually even stronger because they're so risk averse. They're so bootstrapped, and they've had to carry the stuff on their backs and put their own dollars into it. They don't have access to friends and family dollars to raise that initial seed round. These are folks that have had to work way harder, way more meticulously, be way more careful. That's exactly who you want. That's the resilient investment that you want to make."[31]

Up until now, diversity and inclusion tactics have been about getting different kinds of people in the door, and then asking them to assimilate to the dominant white colonizer culture. But the issue is not recruitment of diverse humans—the "pipeline" focus of the past, laying a seat at the table, as is often said—the issue is creating a culture of respect, curiosity, acceptance, and love. It's about fundamentally changing organizational culture, what constitutes acceptable behavior, and the definitions of success and leadership. It's about building ourselves a whole new table—one where we truly belong.

CHAPTER FOUR

Field Hands

How granting funds and loans to those who seek it can feel good . . . but still reinforce colonial dynamics

One day a woman seeking funding for a domestic violence shelter arrived at the Kate B. Reynolds office for a meeting with me. Because she had come from so far away, the other side of the state practically, she had driven to Winston-Salem the day before our appointment and spent the night in a hotel in order to meet with me the next day. I didn't know that, or anything about her or the organization, because at that point we didn't do any screening on the phone. Unless someone was a previous grantee, I walked in blind, with no history or information. I would see that process change during my tenure, but for this woman, those changes hadn't come soon enough. I felt just terrible when this woman said that she had driven up the previous day and spent the night at a hotel. We could have had a 10-minute phone call to determine whether she was eligible instead and saved her the hassle.

To put grantseekers at ease, I usually started with casual conversation. I tried to get on their wavelength. I might talk a little more "country" with them, depending on where in the state they were from. I asked her how the drive had been and she said, "I left the hotel two hours ago to make sure I didn't get lost in this big city, Winston-Salem. Then I got in a car wreck."

From bad to worse. "I am so sorry," I said. "Are you okay?"

"Actually, I feel like I hurt my back," she told me. "I'm in some pain, but I wasn't going to miss this appointment with you, Mr. Edgar."

Oh God, this was terrible. Worse yet, the minute she started talking about the work she was doing and what she was seeking funding for, I knew it was something that we didn't fund. It was tragic. I heard her out anyway and tried to figure out if I could send her on to any other foundations, to make the whole catastrophic trip worth her time.

As we were wrapping up, she looked up at the wall and saw my diploma from Jackson College of Ministries.

"I didn't know that you were a minister."

"Well, I'm not really," I told her, "but I did go to seminary."

She was not taking no for an answer. "No, you are a minister. I knew there was something about you." She started getting excited. "Can I ask you a favor? Will you lay hands on me and pray for my back? I believe God can use you right now, and my back can be healed."

Of course I said yes. There was nothing I wouldn't have done for this woman given the situation, no matter how uncomfortable it made me. Thankfully I already had the door to the office closed because she was a loud talker. So I now stretched out my hand and placed it on her arm, but she took my hand and moved it to the top of her head. *Dear God, don't let anyone walk in my office right now.* I was worried the secretary would come and stick her head in to say my next appointment was there.

Loud enough so she could hear, but as quietly as possible to prevent my colleagues from hearing, I prayed: "Dear God, I pray that you help this sister, and you take this pain away. Let there be a speedy recovery."

She started praying with me, affirming as I spoke. "Yes, Lord. Yes, Lord! Yes, Lord!!" She got louder and louder and louder.

I wanted her to be free of that pain, but I was freaking out about someone coming in and seeing me laying my hands on this woman like a zealous evangelist at a tent revival. Then she started really feeling the Spirit. She literally started shaking and began to have a full, flat-out Holy Ghost visitation right there in my office. I recognized it from my Pentecostal upbringing. She may have even spoken in tongues, I don't remember. Tears streamed down her face.

"YES, JESUS!" she shouted.

Finally the moment subsided and she got ready to go.

At least she got the Spirit, I thought with relief, since she wasn't getting a grant. That was something. Maybe God did use me in that moment to facilitate her healing. Doing that work there were moments I felt I was operating in the flow or in the Spirit. Usually, it was when I could give people money they desperately needed.

~~~

When I arrived, that was the process at Kate B. Reynolds. There was an open invitation for organizations from the state of North Carolina to apply. That sounded good at first, open and fair. But KBR required that people meet with us in person before they applied. They had to come to us like we were the Wizard of Oz bestowing gifts. There was no telephone screening first to help determine eligibility. Most days at the office were filled with back-to-back meetings with these folks seeking funding. There was a waiting area, and although it was of course finely furnished and comfortable, it was awkward for people to see each other there, given they were essentially competing against one another for funding.

The foundation divided responsibilities by geography: each of the program officers covered part of the state. I handled approximately 80 grants per cycle—or per docket, as we say in the biz. My days were filled with meeting, meeting, meeting, meeting, meeting, and then deciding on a slew of grants. I had to pull multiple long weekends to write up my recommendations. It was a lot of work.

I had power in the selection process, basically making a recommendation on who should get funded or not get funded. If I wanted to say no, I could find a way. If you didn't complete your application, I could deliberately not follow up with you to get the rest of the material. If I really wanted to fund you, but you didn't do a good job answering the questions, I could call and dig for more information. I could do the extra work to try to get it to a yes. I searched out organizations and people in the community who were really doing great work. I had the power to help them navigate the system.

I put together the short list and then presented, or sometimes defended, my decision in front of the team, my president, and our advisory board. The executive board, mostly employees of then-Wachovia (now Wells Fargo Bank), had the final approval of all grants, as the bank was the sole corporate trustee. Our advisory board members were all white, and all but one were men. Many of them were also grantees, representatives of large health care systems. That kind of conflict of interest is fairly run of the mill in the world of philanthropy, I would come to learn. If we had a grant pending to a board member's institution, which we pretty much did every cycle, of course we would fund that.

In general, because of our culture of politeness, and out of respect for the due diligence that the staff had done, the board rarely would say no to the staff's recommendations. Between the Southern culture and the philanthropy culture, there was a lot of niceness, no rocking the boat. I learned how to present my recommendations in a way that was compliant, and that was really the only thing they cared about—compliance. *Don't break the law* was essentially their guiding principle. There wasn't a whole lot of pushback.

Still, there were several times where I really wanted to fund something, and I knew their heart was in the right place, but I just could not sell it. The grantseekers didn't give me enough, or it was a little bit too much of a stretch for the foundation's culture. I routinely brought those kinds of proposals in, if only to create the space to have the conversation and to try to push their thinking. One time they overturned a grant that I had recommended for a yes, for an organization that was doing advocacy work. When you went to the organization's website, it screamed lobby and legislation, and it scared the board, so they overturned it. I guess I can't blame them for that one.

The hardest part of the job was having to say no to someone seeking funding for truly good work in their community, based on the sometimes arbitrary rules and regulations of the foundation. I learned over time that I had to be careful about the signs I gave folks, even unconsciously.

As Chris Cardona of the Ford Foundation put it:

> I've come to learn—sometimes the hard way —the weight that your words carry as a philanthropy professional. As informally and accessibly as you try to carry yourself, I've experienced that folks interpret what you're saying and parse it for signals about potential funding. If you're not careful, that can produce disappointment or even harm. That gives me a different kind of pause than I had before. It's probably fair to say that makes me more risk averse with how I communicate. Even to highlight one particular grantee's work can send a signal that I didn't intend. Given the volume of requests, inquiries, and interest we receive as philanthropy professionals, it takes an adjustment to manage relationships responsibly, to manage expectations. It ends up being a big part of the work, both externally and internally.[1]

What Seeking Funds Feels Like

Imagine going to the doctor and explaining at length your symptoms and the gravity of your situation. Your condition is hard to classify, involving intersections of body, mind, and environment, but the doctor forces you to choose a single label for it even though it's not accurate. You have to fill out a pile of paperwork. Finally the doctor sends you away, saying, "Okay, we're going to review your case and decide *if* we will help you." As you leave, you eye the crowd of afflicted people in the waiting room, knowing that only some of the people will get help. In this intense climate of scarcity and competition, you can't help but look at some of them and think, *They don't seem that sick at all, they don't seem like they need the help as much as I do.* Then you go away with your pain and you wait months for an answer. And if you do get the help, you are made to understand that you will have to display improvements within 12 months. If you don't follow the doctor's extensive and confusing regulations to the letter, you might never get help again.

I interviewed a colleague who worked at Amnesty International, "a mostly white organization that does work mostly on behalf of people of color," she notes. "There's a little bit of savior syndrome baked into the DNA of the entire organization." An African American herself, she was invited into fundraising activities when the organization set out to cultivate more Black donors. "So . . . as a token," she says. She described the weird, uncomfortable dynamics:

> The process of getting funding and reporting back about the results is a draining process. It can be a demeaning process. I've been corrected by a white funder for saying "Black folks" instead of African American or African diaspora. I've been corrected to not say "poor people." I was supposed to say "low income."
>
> When it comes time for a site visit from a funder, I have to stand there and smile and speak to the experience of Black folks, shucking and jiving. That's what we say when site visits come up. It's time to shuck and jive. There's something about site visits and the questions that funders ask that isn't always about the work. It doesn't feel like a space to talk honestly about what's working well and what isn't

working well, because the risk that comes with being totally honest and transparent is losing funding.

Fundraising takes our time away from the work and it sometimes subtly and not so subtly directs our work. We have to walk the line between trying to get funders to feel good about funding the work that we're already doing on the one hand, and making sure that funders feel like they're funding the work that they want to fund. It can be a tough line to walk, and the pressure, the burden is on us and not on the funders, so it doesn't really feel like the partnership that they claim it is.

Program officers, because they're not really ever on the ground in the community that they're funding, they don't know who's legitimate and who's not legitimate. Who should be getting the money? Who's really doing the work versus which organizations are writing really great reports with lots of pictures, but they aren't moving the dial? The reality is that healing communities and building power, it takes time, and that doesn't fit with their ideal return on investment.[2]

None of this was news to me. I've heard it from countless grantees. It shouldn't be news to any funder, if they're listening. (Hint: They're not listening.)

Like all investors, foundations have their logic models, their strategic plans, and their theories of change, all of which are too often not applicable to the real world. They believe what they want to believe. Fund seekers are forced to play games, dangling projects that they know have "sex appeal" or reflect the trendy buzz-word of the moment, in order to entice foundations to fund them. Many foundations simply will not fund an organization's existing work. For a long time funders have also leaned away from general operating support—always the most helpful type of grant because it can be applied to all facets of an organization's work as opposed to a single program—although this has finally been shifting in recent years.

It is rare that a funder acknowledges intersectionality: the fact that institutions and identities consist of and are impacted by overlapping and interconnected systems of oppression and disadvantage. Most funding is still stuck in issue-based silos. An education foundation will only fund education, a health foundation will only fund health, and so on, even though we know that every complex social problem has its roots everywhere—the environment, urban design, schools, diet, access to transport, as well as historical and cultural factors. Nevertheless, those seeking funds must still bend over backwards to fit themselves into a foundation's funding area.

A lot of foundations are lazy, funding the usual suspects, which most often are white-led organizations adept at creating glossy promotional materials and/or whose leaders have extensive Rolodexes that grant them more access to funders. The funding process is plagued by the cult of personality. "Funders have traditionally preferred the narrative of a rock star leader, and have invested in individuals more than in missions," comments adrienne maree brown in her book *Emergent Strategy*. "The shiny stars are rarely the ones actually getting the work done, or even doing the most exciting thinking in the organization. If you are in the funding world and your primary relationship with those you fund is with the executive director, if you have not had a meaningful conversation with other staff members or community members, you may be stricken with charismitis—relational laziness induced by charismatic brilliance."[3]

Many groups that are actually based in disadvantaged communities and led by locals are told: "You don't have the data; you don't have the track record; you're not big enough; you're not scalable; you don't align with the strategies we crafted after spending two years on strategic planning," as Vu Le puts it.[4]

As another colleague said, "We hide behind this idea that we're being rigorous and being objective in our grant review, really at the same time creating barriers for smaller organizations, for people-of-color-led organizations. For example, when we ask, 'Does the organization have more than three months of cash on hand? What organizations are going to be more likely to have those resources?' These are things that we do that actually perpetuate inequity."[5] Laborious applications and reporting requirements also keep some worthy groups from applying.

In 2004, the Applied Research Center, a racial justice think tank now known as Race Forward, found that grants aimed at communities of color averaged between 9 and 10 percent of all foundation funding in the 1990s.[6] In 2014, only 7.4 percent of all philanthropy (from individuals as well as institutions) was given for people of color, while foundation funding focused on reaching people of color has never exceeded 8.5 percent, according to the Philanthropic Initiative for Racial Equity.[7] The proportion of money given specifically for African Americans and Natives actually decreased between 2005 and 2014. Despite changing demographics and increased societal awareness of the impacts of systemic racism, there has been no progress on expanding funding for people of color. A 2009 Foundation Center study of New York City foundations found that only 16 percent of them—in the incredibly diverse city of New York!—even had goals or guidelines regarding grantmaking to organizations serving people of color.[8]

Although there's a lot of talk about collaboration between grantees—combining forces rather than duplicating efforts—it's still relatively rare that a foundation explicitly funds it, and funds it adequately. Foundations aren't providing "glue funding" to help hold coalitions together, because it takes extra work to make collaborative decisions, to attend all the coalition meetings, and to loop everyone in.

Finally, there's the absurd contradiction that grantmakers tend to be very slow in collecting proposals and making their funding decisions, on the one hand—although there are occasionally flare-ups of "rapid response grants" in the wake of disasters—while on the other hand, they expect grantees to be able to show outcomes within a year or, at most, several years. Given the complexity of many issues that may have their origin in centuries' worth of root causes, this expectation is just plain crazy.

~~~

KBR was a traditional place. The president was filling the shoes of a beloved longtime predecessor. She won my deepest respect when she started systematically changing the culture. She started redecorating the place not long after she arrived, painting the white walls purple, changing the blinds to colorful window treatments, replacing the heavy antique furniture with modern pieces. There was a lot of gasping and clutching of pearls in response. It may sound superficial, but it was symbolic of the larger cultural changes that ultimately had deep impacts on the community.

We brainstormed changes in the process around how we funded and who we funded. As a program officer, I took care of implementing the strategy changes in the day-to-day work. The president was ultimately the person who had to sell it to the board. I didn't envy her that role. It must have been incredibly stressful, especially since she was the first woman in that position.

One big shift was to move a percentage of the money we granted into preventative health care, away from treatment. Essentially, we wanted to move away from the focus on hospitals and large institutions that had access to capital and focus on other levers of change that impacted health. It was hard to get excited about giving $200,000 for an emergency room at Duke University Medical Center toward their $10 million budget. Duke was going to get there without us. Instead, we wanted to focus our investment more at the root cause of health problems, whether that was obesity prevention, cessation of smoking, or domestic violence prevention. We also wanted to fund smaller community-based organizations led by local leaders, often people of color, that developed specific, customized solutions inside their local communities.

It wasn't easy to make that change; it didn't go over without a fight. The head of the North Carolina Hospital Association—the state lobby for hospitals—was on our advisory board, and he objected when we said we wanted to pull away from funding so many hospitals. He pounded the table with his fists and yelled, "The charter of this foundation says to fund hospitals. We are moving away from its intent."

The foundation's leadership and I also worked to shift the foundation's transactional way of doing business and make it more relational. There were many small local groups doing wonderful work that were not applying to KBR for whatever reason—we needed to reach them. When I came on board, the program officer job description entailed mostly reading proposals and making recommendations. It was completely transactional. I asked permission to rewrite the job descriptions. I wanted the work to be about engaging the community, going out to find excellent groups that were not on our radar, with a goal of bringing in three to five new proposals per docket.

I remember the president asked me, "You want to be held accountable for that?"

"Yes."

So we did it. We changed the job descriptions and actually put program officers on the road.

Previously, as I mentioned, grantseekers had to come to us. There was no screening beforehand: as a grantseeker you would just call and say, "I'm from such and such organization, I'd like to make an appointment." Except for the ones in the good old boys network, grantseekers and even prior grantees who came to our office were nervous, like it was a job interview. When the good old boys came in, we would slap backs and drink tea and exchange gossip and talk about their work, or I might drive over to Duke University, where a fruit basket and flowers waited in my hotel room, and eat a steak lunch with the senior executives.

As KBR moved away from the good old boys network and opened the doors more for small grassroots groups and communities of color, the dynamic changed. Rather than having them come to our offices on the imposing, intimidating Reynolda campus, we went to them, after screening them first on the phone for basic eligibility. This entailed my driving out into rural North Carolina, spending hours on the road and staying at the Hampton Inn hotel, far from glamorous.

I appreciated KBR for being willing to make those strategic changes, to get out of the ivory tower into the community and take a risk on some new grantees. However, none of the changes we made did anything about the core dynamics: The basis of traditional philanthropy is to preserve wealth and, all too often, that wealth is fundamentally money that's been twice stolen, once through the colonial-style exploitation of natural resources and cheap labor, and the second time through tax evasion. Mostly white saviors and experts use this hoarded wealth to dominate and control—obviously or subtly—the seekers and recipients of those funds.

Dynamics of Power

The power dynamic is essentially the same among other kinds of lenders and investors, where the diversity numbers look even worse than in philanthropy. Among borrowers, minorities seeking loans are more heavily scrutinized, while they are given less support and assistance than their white peers. Minority-owned firms are three times more likely to be denied loans (42 percent) than white-owned firms (16 percent), and average loan amounts for minority-owned firms ($149,000) were nearly half of average loans for white-owned firms ($310,000), according to the Minority Business Development Agency of the U.S. Department of Commerce in 2010.[9] And this despite the Community Reinvestment Act of 1977 that requires lending in low-income communities.

Even with "friends and family funding," the support that comes early in the game, when things are still at the crazy idea stage, there are disparities. Those supporters are relatives but also come from alumni groups, professional connections, and social networks. Friends and family funding "accounts for more than $60 billion in small business investment every year. In fact, 38 percent of startup founders report raising money from their friends and family, with each venture raising capital of $23,000 on average," says Jessica Norwood of the Runway Project.[10] Unless, that is, you're talking about entrepreneurs of color. "On average, African American families have $11,000 in net worth, while white families have $141,900. As a result, the great ideas of many African American entrepreneurs never leave the napkin, because their networks simply can't provide the funds to launch a business," Jessica says. "Under current economic conditions, it would take 228 years for the average African American family to accumulate the wealth of an average white family today."[11]

Daryn Dodson, formerly a funds manager at Calvert Funds and now the managing partner of Illumen Capital, which does impact investing, has looked at the bias in investing. He collaborated with Jennifer Eberhardt, the MacArthur "Genius" Grant-winning psychologist who uncovered racial bias in the justice system. She found that bias began at school, where Black boys were being expelled at four times the rate of their white peers for the exact same infractions, contributing to the education gap between races. Dodson found the same thing happening in investment.

When it comes to venture capital financing, the disparities are even starker: only 1 percent of VC funds went to African American and Latino entrepreneurs.[12] In the social finance "doing well by doing good" space, which focuses on ventures that benefit people and solve social or environmental challenges first, and making a profit second, the crowd is overwhelmingly white.

"The white folks in social finance feel more comfortable investing in some sustainable opportunity in Africa than they feel investing in African Americans," commented an African American consultant I chatted with at the 2017 SOCAP conference, the largest gathering in the social finance space. "There's an overlord mentality: they don't trust Black or brown entrepreneurs to handle money. Instead they move the money through one of the intermediary organizations in this space, which are mostly white-led. We've seen some of these white-led intermediaries actually steal the ideas of non-white entrepreneurs and launch it themselves. The young white dude could just make a couple calls, steal the intellectual capital and claim it for himself, and raise money just like that."[13]

At the same time, higher interest rates and worse quality loans tend to go to people of color. "African-American and Latino borrowers were about 30 percent more likely to receive the highest-cost subprime loans relative to white subprime borrowers with similar risk profiles," noted the Center for Responsible Lending, while "African Americans and Latinos are, respectively, 47 percent and 45 percent more likely to be facing foreclosure than whites. . . . As a result of the disproportionate number of foreclosures borne by African Americans and Latinos, the 'spillover' costs, in the form of depreciated home values, increased crime rates, and community blight, are likely to hit communities of color particularly hard."[14]

Ryan Bowers cofounded an organization applying shareholder activism strategies with municipal bonds. Because investment in municipal bonds is a tax-saving strategy, it's usually wealthy people who invest in them. "In a state like, let's say, Alabama," Ryan tells me, "most of the bond investors are mostly old, white, rich men. Municipal bonds are 15 to 20 percent of their total portfolio. They refuse to invest, for example, in Historically Black Colleges and Universities (HBCUs)." The same thing happens in border towns, he says. "Particularly in Texas or other border states, they don't want to invest in the municipal bonds of places that serve a lot of immigrants or potentially undocumented immigrants." As a result of this, "these municipalities have to pay more when they go to the bond market. It takes a longer time for them to find investors, and those bonds sit in the inventory of their brokers longer. It's totally unfair. There's no real laws or framework protecting against that."[15]

Municipal bonds for Native tribal governments are the most restricted, in what Ryan calls an "overseer relationship" with the federal government. When tribes want to pave roads, build housing, or launch other economic development projects, they are not simply permitted to issue bonds for that work as any non-Native municipality in the country is, they have to get permission from the feds. "HBCUs are experiencing redlining in the municipal bond market, but tribal colleges don't even have municipal bonds. There's no investment going into them," says Ryan.

Ryan transitions from there to enlightening me about the role of ratings agencies. They define risk and do underwriting by looking at a city's general fund balance, the debt service ratio. "People talk about philanthropy being like a shadow government, well, the ratings agencies are really the shadow. They have so much power over the cost of capital for a city. They look at the percentage of non-white people in the community: for them that is an indicator of more people on welfare and people who are going to have antisocial behavior and increase your costs. The Fair Lending Act and other civil rights legislation that protects lenders hasn't really made it to the municipal finance market yet."

Ryan and his colleagues worked in Ferguson, Missouri, in 2014 after the police murdered Michael Brown, a Black teenager, which led to protests and a militarized response from the police. "Essentially the credit ratings agencies, the municipal credit ratings agencies, annuities, and Standard and Poors, they ended up downgrading Ferguson's bonds rating, saying they're not going to be able to service their debt and or honor these new obligations. Once Ferguson's bond rating got downgraded the cost of borrowing was going to go through the roof for the next 10 years. Everything was going to cost more, more in interest, more in underwriting fees. They were actually making the city pay for it."[16]

Across the board, among all institutions of finance and wealth, the fundamental dynamic is that control remains in the hands of the old boys' network. Mostly white saviors and experts use hoarded wealth to dominate and control—obviously or subtly—the seekers and recipients of those funds. Our means and mechanisms perpetuate the very problems in the world we claim to wish to solve.

CHAPTER FIVE

The Overseers

What happens when the power and privilege conferred by access to money lead to the savior complex and destructive colonial-style leadership

After several years at Kate B. Reynolds, managing a sizable high-impact portfolio that began to receive some national attention in the field, I was invited to serve on the boards of several organizations. I won some awards and fellowships. The most prestigious came from Grantmakers in Health, which selected me to be among the very first class of Terrance Keenan Institute Fellows. Terrance Kennan, who was affectionately known as Terry, had been one of the first staff members at the health-focused powerhouse: the Robert Wood Johnson Foundation. In his monograph on philanthropy, *The Promise at Hand*, he wrote: "A great foundation is informed and animated by moral purpose. . . . A great foundation walks humbly with its grantees—it acknowledges that their success is the instrument of its own success."[1] Terry's obituary on March 7, 2009, in the *New York Times* noted:

Terry set the standard for creativity, caring and vision in philanthropy. What made Terry so special is that he never lost sight of the people we are trying to help. His modus operandi was to always remember that the Foundation represents a public trust.[2]

A yearlong program, the fellowship focused on leadership development. We were the cream of the crop in health philanthropy, folks who were positioned to move into executive positions in the next three to five years. Everything was going so well for me.

It was at this point that I started getting the sense that some did not like the attention that I was receiving.

One day my boss came into my office and told me, "The way that you're working is making the other program officers feel bad. They've been coming to me saying you're on all these boards, and you're looked at as a leader. They're not on boards. I just think that maybe you shouldn't be on boards." Her stance was that all program officers should be the same and that the experience from the communities' perspective should be consistency— like the service you get from McDonald's.

I was very close with two of the other program officers, both of whom were white women and older than I was. We had lunch together every day. We talked about everything. We hung out outside of work and are still friends to this day. So directly after my boss's comment, during lunch, I asked them outright, "Am I making y'all feel bad?"

"We have no idea what you're talking about," they protested. "We wouldn't say that. We're so proud of your leadership."

I was utterly confused. My boss had always been my mentor. I was her person—the first one she'd hired herself on the staff. We'd made a great team: I implemented her strategies; I was her agent of change.

Serving on boards was a professional development opportunity that not only raised my profile but also the foundation's. And I wasn't neglecting my work at KBR—I was as much of an overachiever as the day I'd arrived six years prior.

I attempted to raise the issue with her, to tell her I'd checked in with the other program officers and discovered they had no objections, but she interpreted this as insubordination. She told me I needed to work on my ability to receive feedback.

Despite the fact that it made no sense, I was forced to resign from all my board positions. I began to feel like I was being told to keep my head down. I felt silenced.

Then, at a meeting in front of our entire board of directors, she remarked offhand, jokingly, but one of those jokes with a razor-sharp serious edge under it, "Edgar, you are getting too big for your britches!"

For those of you needing a translation of this Southern idiom, this statement is a phrase of ridicule used as far back as the sixteenth century, meaning that my assumed position or sense of importance was exaggerated or larger than the position I'd been granted. The phrase is meant to diminish, oppress, or even threaten someone who may be esteeming himself too highly. It insinuates the need for an adjustment.

Not long after, she called me into her office and asked, "Edgar, where do you want to be in five years?"

"Well, I think I want to be the CEO of a foundation one day."

She nodded. "I thought so." And then she said, "I want to help you. Let's figure out a plan. You're too big for KBR. You should be at Ford, Kellogg, somewhere. Let's get you out of here and to positions that are going to get you where you need to go."

I was so grateful. She was very well connected, a former executive coach. We set my departure date as one year from that meeting and I began applying for jobs— program officer positions at bigger foundations, or vice president positions, one step up from where I was. Often we'd do a mock interview together before to prepare me for the interviews.

Still, I didn't get any job offers.

During this time, KBR held a capacity building training for our grantees, way out in the far east side of the state. We brought in a nationally known consultant to lead it. He was very well regarded and professional. After the training, as I was driving him to the airport, he told me he had heard I was leaving the foundation.

"This is really uncomfortable for me to say," he said, "but I just feel like I need to tell you this. I think that you're trusting the wrong people with your career. I can't say too much, but I think you should just start keeping things to yourself and not telling people."

What the heck was he talking about? Who was he talking to? What was happening?

I was thoroughly confused by this conversation, and on the long drive back to Winston-Salem, I decided to call my mentor, who worked at the University of North Carolina at Chapel Hill. I had recently applied for a director-level position at the school. I was in the final running for the job; I was excited about the opportunity.

He answered his phone on the first ring. "Where are you right now?"

I told him the exit I'd just passed.

"Oh my God, take the next exit." It was eerie, almost supernatural, that we were in the same place, both so far from home, at the same moment. I pulled off at the following exit and we followed each other into a McDonald's parking lot. We went in, ordered some drinks, and sat down.

"I need to talk with you about something," he began. "Know I did not want to tell you this. This is terrible, but I feel like there's a reason you called me, and why we were both right here. I have to tell you this. I know you're in an extremely competitive position for the job at the University of North Carolina (UNC) at Chapel Hill. Someone from the foundation called me."

Other than me, he didn't even know folks at the foundation well—definitely not well enough to receive this kind of call. And no one there knew that that he and I knew each other, that we were in fact very close.

"They called me and said, 'Look, I need to tell you some stuff about Edgar. Y'all would be making a huge mistake if you hired him.'"

He went on, describing how they had made me out to be a severely problematic person, practically a monster.

I told him that made no sense at all, that the leadership of the foundation had literally been coaching me through the job search process. Why would anyone say awful things about me behind my back?

"You have got to shut it down."

I literally wept as I drove back to Winston-Salem. Beyond the job thing, I was personally devastated.

I didn't know how to handle it. My future was in the hands of the foundation. KBR gave a lot of money to everyone, including UNC. Even if people didn't believe what was said about me, no one in the state was going to endanger their relationship with the foundation by hiring me. The evaporation of trust was torturous because I loved my work at the foundation and loved and respected the leadership. I didn't want to say anything bad about it or anything bad about the leadership. I had understood that it was my time to go, and I was leaving, but could I just land a new job first? I mean, I had a mortgage, thanks to Oprah. Ultimately, I had to keep my job search process a secret. I'd just give vague updates when asked.

I faced the threat of going back into poverty. I couldn't get a job. I was terrified that my life was going to fall apart. I became physically ill, highly anxious, and unable to eat. I developed irritable bowel syndrome. My hair started falling out, a stress-related condition called alopecia. I had to go into therapy. I went to .pastoral counseling. I asked people who prayed seriously to pray for me. In the end I moved my departure date up, and I left the foundation early without even having a job lined up. I just knew that I had to get out of there.

Eating Our Own

I left out something about my boss at KBR in telling you my story: she is African American. While I was living through it, this fact made the situation all the more heartbreaking, but in retrospect, it's also allowed me to find compassion and forgiveness. She was not only the first woman to ever hold that leadership position at KBR, she was the first Black person. As a Black woman, she took it upon herself to challenge the status quo of the foundation and its good old boys board and community network. I can't fully imagine what kind of pressure she was under or how she may have suffered. I can imagine how she may have felt when I began to get more attention and shine brighter. When I told her that my aspiration was to become the head of a foundation myself, that could have been the final straw. Maybe my ambition was too unbridled.

Over the years I've seen really terrible behavior between people of color within philanthropy, I believe because the space for us feels so limited. Inside these privileged, powerful places that are almost entirely white, occasionally a "designated space" opens up for you as a person of color, a token. Quite possibly you've never had access to power and all of a sudden, you're going to these fancy dinners and having meetings with CEOs and mayors. There is a sense of specialness and scarcity, that there's only a few of us who get in the door, and so you want to hold on to your spot and to the little bit of power and privilege that you have. All of a sudden there's another person of color. You almost can't help being afraid that person might take it all away from you. It can make us behave terribly toward one another. Some of my friends call this the "shiny new penny syndrome."

While I had hoped that she and other leaders would celebrate my accomplishments as a Southern Native American working in institutional philanthropy, I have had to push through diminishment and oppression at every turn of my professional life for the past decade— usually from leaders from whom I sought support and guidance.

Later, after a break from philanthropy following my departure from KBR, I heard about an interesting opportunity at a foundation in Seattle. It was about as far in the opposite direction as I could go and still be in the field of philanthropy. I don't mean geographically, although that was also true. Unlike the Southern tobacco dynasty rooted in slavery, the money behind this new foundation came from a classic entrepreneurial American rags-to-riches story. In 1899, in Seattle, 11-year-old Jim Casey had to drop out of school to find work because of his father's failing health. Jim was the eldest of the four Casey kids. He started out as a delivery boy for a department store earning $2.50 per month. When he was 19, he borrowed $100 to cofound a small messenger service with a buddy. "It consisted of six messengers, two bicycles, and a telephone, operating from a 6- by 17-foot basement of a saloon." It was the Little Engine that Could, and it grew and it grew until it became the world's largest package delivery company, UPS. Several foundations focused on the well-being of families and children were created with the resulting wealth.[3]

In contrast to KBR, this foundation operates nationwide, espousing some of the most explicitly progressive values you can find in philanthropy. They cite transparency and accountability, equity, mutual trust and respect, and antiracism among their guiding values. Their grantees are organizations doing some of the smartest, most innovative work to address the root causes of poverty, inequality, and discrimination.

And yet! In this new foundation I experienced what I perceived to be another case of internalized oppression, far more nefarious than my experience at KBR. Even today, having left there and moved on to another foundation in New York City, I still fear the potential reprisals that would come from sharing all the details of the situation. This is what the power of the overseer can do. Have you seen Miranda Priestly in *The Devil Wears Prada*? Yeah.

Here, alliances had sprung up between the grantees themselves and the grantmaking staff as the controlling, overseer-type behavior was well known and had been experienced by many. The grantees had actually learned to look out for the staff, to support them, to say whatever they needed to say to keep their program officers in good favor, thereby protecting their internal ally for future funding. Most of the grantees had learned the art of flattering my boss in order to keep the checks coming, because she had the power to approve all grants—every penny. Organizations were added and removed from the docket with no explanation, leaving us program officers to come up with some halfway believable reason. The act of funding so many stellar organizations had created delusions of grandeur and a definite entitlement in the foundation's leadership, who by the end of my tenure was pursuing its own political organization with the idea of it ultimately becoming the largest organization in America to fight on behalf of poor families. Everyone was terrified to tell the empress that she had no clothes, for fear of retaliation that could diminish funding to the grantees.

The staff was kept at a distance in order to control the narrative with the board. It wouldn't do for them to question the leadership's judgments about the staff and our work, or decisions about firing and restructuring. Many dozens of people had come and gone through this foundation, and it was less than a decade old. Tragically, the leadership style absolutely embodied the mantra of colonizers: *divide, control, and above all, exploit.*

I had thought the leadership at KBR was a tragic example of internalized oppression, but this place would take it to a whole other level, where the hunger for power seemed to have no limits. And I am far from alone in having had these kinds of terrible experiences with the very people I would most have hoped to be supported by.

~~~

A year after the first Terry Keenan fellowship ended, all of us who had been in that first class convened to check in and catch up with each other. When I started counting the changes, something like 23 percent of us no longer worked in philanthropy. Why were 23 percent of the field's supposed brightest stars no longer working in philanthropy?

When I asked the fellows why they left, people had their own camera-ready responses, things like "I wanted a more authentic relationship with community," or "I just felt like it was the time for a transition for me." I dug deeper, and I started calling people one-on-one, and I shared my story. What I found out was almost every single person had the same story as me.

We lacked role models and mentors: people who looked like us. We lacked access to informal networks that translated to power. We were limited by stereotypes and preconceptions of our aptitudes and cutting edges. We were pushed out because we were not status quo. We were pushed out because we were asking the hard questions about "underserved populations" (code for Black and brown folks). We were pushed out when the leadership, be it boards or bosses, could not handle our gifts and made us miserable until we left. We were treated as disposable. We were treated with no sense of dignity.

One of the darkest, most insidious results of the trauma of racism and colonization is internalized oppression. Here we all are, Natives and people of color and white people, living together inside a complex global system that has normalized treating certain kinds of people as less than worthy, even questioning their right to exist—from immigrants to Indigenous, from people with disabilities to people of color, from women and girls to queer folk to people holding low-status jobs. When you live inside a system like this, breathing the air, drinking the water, watching the television, it is beyond easy—in fact, it's almost a given—that you'll absorb the cultural attitudes, myths, and stereotypes; you'll be affected by it and infected by it. Internalized oppression involves consciously or unconsciously adopting the mindset of the exploiter, the oppressor, the hater.

Because it's generally not safe to lash out against the actual perpetrators, this kind of behavior plays out where it is "safe," which, tragically, means turning this mindset toward yourself or toward members of your own group—especially those over whom you have some degree of control. You perpetuate the abusive treatment that you received at the hands of those who diminished, exploited, and abused you. You turn it against your already wounded self and your fellow wounded. Internalized oppression is heartbreaking.

With yourself, internalized oppression may manifest as inferiority, inadequacy, self-hatred, self-invalidation, self-doubt, isolation, fear, feelings of powerlessness, and despair. You might drive yourself into the ground in a quest for perfection and acceptance, or the opposite, you might throw in the towel and stop showing up for school or for work. You might develop compulsive behaviors, eating disorders, addictions. You might walk around loudly protesting that exploitation and oppression of people like yourself is a total myth. You might get stuck in one abusive relationship after another. You might suffer from depression, or have intense, disruptive outbursts of bitterness or anger. All of these behaviors map onto internalized oppression.

Around others, it may look like name-calling, stereotyping, or character assassination. You might be rude or dismissive when members of your group dress in a traditional way or otherwise take steps to connect to their heritage. You might psychologically abuse people from your community who have lower status jobs than you in your workplace. You might gossip, backstab, blame.

Internalized oppression can mean we don't respect ourselves, and we cover it with self-righteousness. We toughen our children up and focus on their flaws with the intention of making them invincible. We project our negativity and feelings of powerlessness on our own leaders, who make easy targets. We complain rather than taking responsibility for making things better.

The Savior Dynamic

When I speak to young professionals in philanthropy and finance now, I always tell them, "You have to be careful about the Whitney Houston–Bobby Brown syndrome." When Whitney was married to Bobby Brown, anytime she was in public with him, she declared him the greatest entertainer of all time with a shout and a wave of the hand. It was like she had to diminish herself and publicly announce that he was a bigger star than she was, in order to thrive in that relationship. You can be a leader in the community and outside of the institution, where you can shine bright as a diamond, but you can't steal the spotlight of someone else at your organization who has more power than you—especially if they're occupying one of the few coveted spots for token minorities.

Because of the power associated with controlling wealth, leaders in institutions of philanthropy and finance are some of worst perpetrators of the savior dynamic. Despite all their talk of wanting to help, reform, even revolutionize the world, saviors won't touch the underlying system of privilege and power because that's what grants them their status and position in the world. In the end, saviors don't heal anything. The savior complex often goes hand in hand with white supremacy. Not all saviors are white; some are people of color and Indigenous people who have been infected by the power dynamic of colonization and internalized oppression.

Here's the thing about saviors: No matter how much they think the victim may need their help, rescuing someone can only reinforce their victimhood. There's a theory from psychology around this dynamic called the Drama Triangle. It states that there are three roles in abusive or oppressive situations: perpetrator, victim, and savior. Victims hurt, perpetrators inflict the hurt, and saviors relieve or remove the hurt. These three interlocking roles work together to create cycles of hurt, blame, and guilt that continue endlessly unless we awaken to them.

The key to escaping the Drama Triangle dynamic is to shift from looking for affirmation and purpose externally, outside oneself, from others. Everyone must take full responsibility for her/himself, and learn to cultivate purpose and worth internally, without needing the other players in the power dynamic. When we have transcended the Triangle we embody the "both/and" of the famous quote from Dr. Martin Luther King, Jr.: "Power without love is reckless and abusive, and love without power is sentimental and anemic. Power at its best is love implementing the demands of justice, and justice at its best is love correcting everything that stands against love."[4]

Internalized oppression limits us just as much as the oppression coming from someone else. It limits the thoughts we can think, the dreams we can dream, the actions we can take, the futures we can create. It is an aspect of trauma we must heal from, in order to stop the cycles of division, exploitation, and hurt.

CHAPTER SIX

Freedom

How our focus on individual leaders is also a
reflection of the colonizer virus

It was around the time I left KBR when I got my
Indian name. I wish I could tell you a romantic story
about a vision quest where I became a man after spending a month building my own shelter, sleeping under
the stars, foraging and nearly starving, and having hal-
lucinogenic experiences that revealed the true nature of
things. But that's not how it happened.

No, it was in a beige conference room in the Marriott
Hotel in Denver. I had found a job, finally, in the direct
aftermath of KBR, and was running the North Carolina
American Indian Health Board, an organization that rep-
resented the six tribes around the state, working toward
improved health in our communities, and the National
Indian Health Board conference was taking place in
Denver. There at the conference was a sign-up sheet to
meet with an Ojibwe medicine man.

Obviously, I signed up.

There was a line of people waiting their turn to go
into the room and have a session with him, and I was

nervous. In my church, growing up, this kind of thing—shamans and the like—would have been condemned as heresy.

"What's going to happen in there?" I asked the woman waiting in line in front of me. I felt like I was on my way to see the Great and Powerful Oz.

She looked at me doubtfully and asked, "Do you have tobacco to give him?"

Um. I don't carry around tobacco with me. "Is that what they like?" I asked.

"You have to take a gift!" she said, shocked at my ignorance. She broke off a bit of hers and gave it to me.

I went in, holding the tobacco out in front of me. The medicine man nodded at his assistant to take it from me, and gestured for me to sit down. We sat in generic hotel chairs across from each other at a generic hotel table. He was wearing something vaguely ceremonial but not extravagant. I was wearing my usual colonized attire: as nice a suit as I could afford.

He stared at me for a moment. I felt very uncomfortable, skeptical but hopeful at the same time.

He asked me why I'd come. The truth was someone had suggested that if I were lucky, he might give me an Indian name, even though it's pretty unusual for someone from another tribe to give you a name. There are different traditions around naming. My tribe does not have a naming ceremony. You are just who you are, whatever your mama names you. I felt I'd be more legit with a real Indian name, but of course I wasn't going to express that to the medicine man.

So I said, "I'm part of this organization, trying to help my community. I'm trying to get reconnected to my culture because I did not grow up in traditional Native ways. I just want to open my mind to all of this, so that

I can be in a better position to help my community back in North Carolina." I was babbling a bit.

"The ancestors are happy that you're here," he said.

What? My colonized mind kicked in, wondering if this dude was totally making stuff up. At the same time, I thought I might burst into tears.

He talked about the colors he saw coming from me. His eyes flickered around the room as he spoke, and suddenly he flinched and practically ducked: the ancestors and spirits were flying around the room, he told me.

Okay, this was definitely ridiculous. Wasn't it? I had no idea. I wanted to scream and run out of the room, but I couldn't move, I was transfixed. And then he said it: "I want to give you an Indian name."

My moment had arrived. My prayers had been granted.

Niigaanii Beneshi.

It's in Ojibwe, which was his tribe, from northern Minnesota.

"It means Leading Bird," he added, sparing me from having to find someone who speaks Ojibwe to translate it for me. "When birds are flying in the V-formation, there's a bird that's leading the formation. That's you."

I thanked him and floated out of the room feeling all spiritual and mysterious after the experience. *Niigaanii Beneshi.* Leading Bird.

~~~

After I left him I researched the qualities of migratory birds. It turns out migration is no party: more birds die during migration than at any other time, from dehydration, starvation, or sheer exhaustion. When birds fly together, they cut the wind for each other—all except for the one at the front. That one has to bear the full force of the wind. That one has to stick his nose out. That one has to lead the way forward despite the discomfort.

At the same time, one of the great lessons of migrating birds is that they take turns occupying that tough position at the front, which allows for greater resilience for the whole group. By working together, a flock of birds is greater than the sum of its parts. In her book *Emergent Strategy*, adrienne maree brown writes about what we can learn from flocks of birds:

> There is a right relationship, a right distance between them—too close and they crash, too far away and they can't feel the microadaptations of the other bodies. Each creature is shifting direction, speed, and proximity based on the information of the other creatures' bodies. There is a deep trust in this: to lift because the birds around you are lifting, to live based on your collective real-time adaptations. In this way thousands of birds or fish or bees can move together, each empowered with basic rules and a vision to live.
>
> Imagine our movements cultivating this type of trust and depth with each other, having strategic flocking in our playbooks. Adaptation reduces exhaustion. No one bears the burden alone of figuring out the next move and muscling towards it. There is an efficiency at play—is something not working? Stop. Change. If something is working, keep doing it—learning and innovating as you go.[1]

The lesson is that thriving is not actually about the leader, it's about the whole flock. Everyone has the potential to lead, and leadership is about listening and being attuned to everyone else. It's about flexibility. It's about humility. It's about trust. It's about having fun along the way. It is more about holding space for others' brilliance than being the sole source of answers, more about flexible shape-shifting to meet the oncoming challenges than holding fast to a five-year strategic plan.

I am frequently asked, *What does decolonized leadership look like?* Compassionate, empathetic, vulnerable leaders? Servant leaders? Leaders who listen? Yes, and it's not about the individual. We have to shift from our obsession with individual leaders to a focus on organizational design, which tends to be taken for granted and invisible in most of our institutions.

Fortunately, conversations about new kinds of organizational design have been exploding recently. There's a sea change happening, moving us away from the colonized hierarchical pyramid structure, with its command-and-control leadership, to a realization of how everyone has leadership potential. Businesses have been at the forefront of experimenting with organizational models that transcend the colonized mindset of division, control, and exploitation; now it's time for the fields of philanthropy and finance to follow their lead, in order to heal divides and restore balance.

~~~

The day after I received my name, the Native Health conference ended. As I was heading to my gate at the Denver airport, I saw the medicine man wearing a T-shirt and jeans, eating at TGI Fridays. That's the modern American Indian existence for you. Natives can be both denim-wearing, television-watching, and fast-food-eating people on the one hand, and people who honor the ancestors, participate in ceremonial rituals, and prepare traditional feasts on the other.

I was reminded of an observation from my mentor, a Lumbee elder named Donna Chavis who worked in institutional philanthropy before me, one of the very first Native women to do so. She had been telling stories about her grandfather, "a Bible-thumping Baptist preacher. His way of being was not just Christian; it was a blend, because he was a traditional healer too. He made the connection." As I've mentioned, the contemporary Lumbee identity inevitably includes faith in Christianity, a result of the fact that we were colonized 500-some years ago.

"Blending Native tradition with Christianity made it possible to move through both worlds. There was not a rejection—it was not either/or—it was *both/and*. The *both/and* mindset influenced just about everything in the way I was raised within our clan. I think the word *mutual* captures it," said Donna. "Mutual means that both sides have something to offer, and that's what's true."[2]

When the both/and disappears and Indigenous people have to choose either the colonizers' way or the traditional way, and reject the other way, including whatever good might exist within it, they tend to be much less resilient. There are studies on alcoholism among Natives, Donna told me, that showed that the Indians who had the highest chance of becoming alcoholics were the ones on either end of the spectrum: those who completely adopted the ways of the colonizers and those who completely rejected them. "It was those who learned *not only* how to respect and live within their culture *but also* to navigate the world outside their culture who wound up having the lower risk of alcoholism," she told me.[3]

Being Native means living in the comple[x] where worlds meet. Members of Native American tribes literally hold dual nationalities: first as citizens of their Native nation, and second as citizens of the United States. Today in our everyday lives we do not dress like Natives portrayed in movies like *Dances with Wolves*. We blend in; we're wearing jeans (or the latest B. Yellowtail fashions) and jet-setting. We're getting degrees in law and Western medicine. At the same time, we've still got a connection to the land we've always lived on, to the places where our ancestors are buried, to our songs and our medicine.

"Integration means we can lift up what we have. At the same time, we bring in what is needed," as Donna says.[4] Accepting the both/and nature of things was key to Indigenous survival against all odds.

By the time I left KBR I was fairly thoroughly colonized, after years of church, mainstream schooling and higher education, and then the oh-so-white experience of the foundation built with tobacco money. It's no coincidence that it was at this point in my story that I really began the process of becoming more curious about my Native heritage and connecting with Indigenous traditions. For modern Natives, the process of decolonization often looks like this: exploration and embrace of traditional rituals and practices from which one has become disconnected.

"The essence of trauma is disconnection from ourselves," says Gabor Maté, a Hungarian-born doctor who is one of the world's top experts on trauma. "Trauma is not terrible things that happen from the other side— those are *traumatic*. But the trauma is that very separation from the body and emotions. So, the real question is, 'How did we get separated and how do we reconnect?'

Because that's our true nature—our true nature is to be connected."[5]

Becoming reconnected—overcoming the mindset of separation—is how humans heal from trauma. Reconnecting can mean remembering traditions and honoring our community's wisdom. It can mean researching our family history and finding out how our wealth was generated. It will probably mean remembering and re-experiencing painful events. I know for me this was the case. There's so much that I had pushed out of my memory, that I had wanted to forget.

Reconnecting might mean having vulnerable, difficult, awkward conversations with people who are harmed by the system we benefit from. It may entail forgiveness of those who have harmed us. It means recognizing that we are part of something greater, that we belong together, that we are all in this thing called life together. This is all part of the path to freedom, to really restoring balance in our lives and in the world.

But—for me at least—it's not simply just a full return to the ancient ways; it's the both/and integration. I have no intention of acquiring traditional skills like hunting and skinning game or building canoes or shelters by hand. I intend to keep working with money, guiding people to think about it as medicine, as a tool of decolonizing and healing. I am keeping my tailored suits (tailored in my head at least!) and my Brooklyn apartment. As they say about relationship status: *It's complicated.*

I firmly believe that integrating my Native heritage has contributed to my resilience when I went on to new roles within philanthropy to encounter even greater challenges. As I've faced off with more overseers, saviors, and my own internalized oppression, I've been able to call upon the aspects of myself that are Lumbee, that are the Leading Bird.

As humanity faces all kinds of challenges that have come from the separation worldview—the devastation of the planet, the hate and fear between different religions and races and political ideologies—cultivating integration will be key to healing and saving all of us and restoring balance to the world.

PART TWO

How to Heal

In order to embrace a new paradigm of *connect, relate, belong*, instead of *divide, control, exploit*, we first have to heal. The metaphor of healing reflects my stance in the reform vs. revolution debate. Some will say that the colonial system of wealth consolidation based on white supremacy has caused so much damage and suffering and is so intrinsically rotten that anything related to it, including the ostensibly altruistic worlds of philanthropy or aid, cannot be fixed, cannot be trusted, should not be saved. Those voices would burn the system to the ground and start fresh. I empathize with that perspective, yet I believe there are parts of the system worth holding on to. The both/and stance is how Native Americans have survived colonization. Evolution occurs both by holding on to the adaptations that keep us thriving, and also abandoning the elements that keep us from thriving.

~~~

Every time we contemplate huge goals like social justice and equity, or a slightly smaller goal like real evolution inside the field of finance or philanthropy, we encounter beliefs about what is possible. What is pragmatic and realistic, and what is idealistic or utopian? I expect that some of the Seven Steps to Healing will be considered radical by large, long-standing institutions. There will be those who say my proposals are too far out there, a fantasy, pie in the sky.

This is the tension that we face in evolving. People who rely on the current system are afraid to dismantle it, because when we're out in the middle of the ocean during the perfect storm, no land in sight, who's going to poke holes in the only lifeboat we have, even if it's a terrible vessel?

There is always this abyss. On one side of it are the pragmatists, saying *this is just the way things are, we have to make the best of it, things never change, it's human nature*. On the other side of the abyss are the idealists, imagining another world, building utopias. Some of the hardest work involves crisscrossing the abyss, understanding both positions, and seeking ways to bridge them. Evolving a complex set of systems, like white supremacy and capitalism, and long-standing institutions like governments, banks, and foundations, requires bridge builders who can envision opportunities for change and lead with compassion.

Marginalization and oppression seem to stifle the imagination—among both those who suffer and those who benefit from the current transactional systems of wealth. Unfortunately, the majority of our groundbreaking and inspiring idealists are part of the powerful elite, holding all the high cards of privilege: think of players like Elon Musk and Richard Branson. We need to populate the idealist side of the abyss with different kinds of people who have different visions of future possibilities.

Much has been written about how colonizers rewrite the history of the places and the people they colonize. Part of keeping total control is staking a claim on the past. But colonizers also control the future. They control what is imaginable.

The idealists yell over the abyss that the sheep stuck in the status quo are cowards. The pragmatists shout back that the idealists are out of touch with reality. One response to the pragmatists is to question their certainty that this is indeed reality. We can be like Neo in *The Matrix* taking the red pill and seeing the constructed world as an illusion. "The willingness to own up to the fictional nature of our story is where the healing begins," writes Peter Block in his book on civic engagement, *Community*.[1]

White supremacy is just a story humans created. Race is just a story humans created. Resources as scarce, greed as an inescapable aspect of human nature, and money as the root of evil—all these are stories. Over time, these stories have become so solidified and familiar and "true" that they began limiting our view of the world and our choices. They became beliefs, articles of faith. Yet our beliefs are just one perspective, and the more rigid our perspective, the more alternative perspectives we miss.

Once we understand that the stories are optional— choices we made—we can choose to let go of any beliefs that limit us. Every obstacle can be incorporated and can become an ally, another beautiful aspect of authentic wholeness. A free imagination is key to overcoming limiting beliefs.

The central question at the foundation of much science fiction—"What if . . .?"—is a legitimate tool of healing and reconstructing the world. Even just asking the question opens us to radically different possible realities and can lead to healing, to a greater sense of dignity and purpose. The film *Black Panther* allowed us to imagine a fictionalized nation of unfathomable wealth that refuses to play by the rules of divide-control-exploit, to imagine a world where Black people triumph. #WakandaForever

What if funders could help restore a perfect world? What if money could be medicine, instead of what divides us? What if rather than using wealth to cause further harm, we followed the Seven Steps to Healing?

Grieve

I t's not what you were expecting from a book about wealth. Yet before we can move forward with using money as medicine, to heal divides and restore balance, we have to grieve. Grieving requires softening your self-protective defense mechanisms enough to feel: getting beyond the denial, numbness, righteousness, apathy, and other obstacles we have put in place to avoid the depths of pain. The humanity that was previously made invisible must be made visible again.

We who were colonized have to grieve for the people, the cultures, and the lands that were forcibly taken from us. We have to mourn the suffering of our ancestors who were cheated, humiliated, raped, and killed. We have to grieve for hundreds of years of our being disrespected, displaced, and dispossessed. We have to grieve for our children, who embody the trauma of this history, and now have the decks stacked against them as they face the future.

Those who have embodied and sustained the colonizer virus also have much to grieve for. The fear, anxiety, and mistrust that characterizes being a member of the 1 percent is no joke. The survival mechanisms they often adopt include staying walled off, physically and emotionally disconnected, and well medicated.

White people have to grieve the guilt that accompanies whiteness. You cannot and must not opt out of whiteness. You have to grapple with the messiness of the privilege. You have to come and collect your people.

Settlers and their descendants have to grieve the lives of their ancestors, the culture that made their acts of domination and exploitation even imaginable, possible, and acceptable. What confused, numbed, dissociated hell it must have been, on a deep level, even if they enjoyed benefits on other levels. Hurting people hurt others (something else I learned growing up watching Oprah). Generations down the line must grieve the culture of the present, which perpetuates the colonizer mindset of domination and exploitation.

Trust me, I know that there are those who are not ready to consider the suffering of colonizers and oppressors, let alone forgive them or welcome them. However, the Native principle of All My Relations means that settlers are our relatives too. It means our interdependence is inescapable, so we may as well acknowledge each other's trauma and engage in healing together.

Stephen Jenkinson, a white Canadian trained in theology at Harvard, best known for his writing and speaking about his work with people who are dying, has also reflected profoundly on what it is to be a non-Indigenous, a settler. He calls it being an "orphan," a term that includes all the people uprooted from their ancestral homes for whatever reasons, whether it was by choice or not. The European settlers who came to the Americas are orphans, but so are the slaves they brought over, and so are the people lured to America's shores in recent decades by the promise of work, wealth, and the American Dream. They are all orphans, in his worldview:

> Orphans are not people who have no parents: they are people who don't know their parents, who cannot go to them. Ours is a culture built upon the ruthless foundation of mass migration, but it is more so now a culture of people unable to say who their people are. In that way we are, relentlessly, orphans.[1]

Orphans broke the ties to their lands of origin, to the bones of their ancestors, to their old ways. The grief that this has caused is enormous, yet it is almost never acknowledged. In the wake of the choice to abandon, to sever, to forget, Jenkinson believes, is shame of secretly believing you come from nothing that has merit. First and foremost, Jenkinson calls for sorrow and grieving among orphans, acknowledging the profound longing for connection and purpose and ancestry.

Reframing colonizer-settlers as orphans and cultivating empathy for them will probably rub some people the wrong way. I get it. It's not just about turning the other cheek, taking the higher road, or being more virtuous, though. It's literally a pragmatic choice in order to end the cycles: the cycles of pain and hurt; the cycles of *divide, control, and above all, exploit.* According to those who work to heal abusers, the point of recognizing the victimization of perpetrators is not to excuse, forgive, or in any way diminish the destructiveness of their actions, but rather to develop an accurate understanding of how oppression works, how it is sustained and recreated over generations, how to end it.

So all of us have to grieve how the culture of domination and exploitation took us over, no matter the color of our skin or how we came to live in this country. We have to grieve what all we've done since being infected with the colonizer virus: how exploitation was at the foundation of how we earned and used and managed money, how transactions replaced relationships, how we lost sight of our common humanity.

In her book *Medicine Stories*, the curandera-historian Aurora Levins Morales writes:

> Ours is a society that does not do grief well or easily, and what is required to face trauma is the ability to mourn, fully and deeply, all that has been taken from us. But mourning is painful and we resist giving way to it, distract ourselves with put-on toughness out of pride. . . . What is so dreadful is that to transform the traumatic we must re-enter it fully, and allow the full weight of grief to pass through our hearts. It is not possible to digest atrocity without tasting it first, without assessing on our tongues the full bitterness of it.[2]

~~~

One of my conversations while writing this book was with Hilary Giovale, a trustee of the Geo Family Foundation. A white woman who became involved in philanthropy after marrying into wealth, she's become something of advocate for awakening other white folks to white privilege, and believes that white people absolutely need to be saved from white supremacy.

Hilary told me:

> About a year and a half ago, I developed an interest in learning about my ancestry, because the story for most of us white folks starts here

in America, with no recollection of what happened before our arrival. My understanding had been that my people had come from Scotland and Ireland several generations ago, and that we were very poor people, seeking a new beginning. Although this is true of my most recent ancestors I now understand that focusing on this story while excluding the big picture is part of the mythology that helps justify white supremacy. I came to realize that I had an ancestor who arrived in 1739 from Scotland and he landed in North Carolina. His grandson received a land grant. I was horrified as it became clear to me that it was land stolen from Indigenous people of North Carolina. Later that grandson went down to Mississippi and Louisiana, and he and some of his descendants owned slaves. There were records of slaves' names and how much they were worth in a book of family genealogy. Again, it was devastating. I had to go through a process of deep grieving.[3]

When we white people start to learn about this history and to build relationships with people who are still living the intergenerational historical trauma of colonization on a daily basis, a lot of us are totally paralyzed by guilt and by shame, and we don't know what to do, so we have to check out. We have to put our blinders on and become numb to all of that. I see that whole dynamic as part of the reason that we're still so separate today. . . . The first thing you have to do is understand that you have white privilege. When you understand that you have it, you are going to feel bad. You're going to feel some discomfort, guilt, and shame. This is part of the process and cannot be short-circuited. Engaging these uncomfortable feelings opens space for different ways of interacting with diverse people and projects. It creates possibilities for healing to happen on all sides.[4]

Philanthropist Peter Buffett talked to me about how it was no coincidence that the first philanthropic organizations were created in the Gilded Age, against the backdrop of industrialization which, alongside creating enormous concentrations of wealth, also led to anxiety, depression, and existential crises. For most people, work had gone from mostly autonomous productive activities that involved a sense of purpose and satisfaction, like craftsmanship or farming, to being a cog in the assembly line of industry somewhere, lacking any sense of agency or power. "It led to 150 years of purposeless, especially for men. The most powerful tried to put a salve on these losses with philanthropy, but the losses were huge. When you unpack this, there's a lot of pain."[5]

~~~

Organizations, companies, and institutions can support the grieving process. Once upon a time this idea would have been laughed at as unprofessional or indulgent, but there is increasing evidence that intentionally creating and holding space for grief can make an organization more productive. Organizational designers now recommend that pain be publicly acknowledged and mourned. Sharing the grief destigmatizes the feelings, validates them, and allows for healing.

The day after the election of Donald Trump in 2016, I was on a flight to Atlanta to attend Facing Race, a national conference of racial justice organizers and advocates. Days before, I had been confident that I was going to be attending a victorious celebration with a thousand of my closest friends in philanthropy and the movement. Instead, we boarded the flight like a funeral procession. We sat soberly, in extreme grief. As we gathered in Atlanta, no one could fathom the country's choice of hateful, backwards-thinking leadership. A roomful of visionaries were unable to see through the tears. We spent those few days together talking through the election results, crying, and beginning to process. It was a lifesaver for me. I can think of no better place to have been in such a time. In the weeks following, I heard stories about how some foundations held space for grieving, while others did not even acknowledge the immense sorrow being carried by staff. In many cases, staff self-organized to hold each other up. Spaces for grief validate us and help to start the process of healing.

An organizational design consultant in post-apartheid South Africa commented how much of the emphasis in institutions is on articulating an exciting vision of the future. But "selling the vision of a new, exciting future to people who are still in grief is akin to telling a grieving husband at the grave of his wife to marvel at the beauty and virtues of potential wives standing around the grave. Such thinking ignores the loss, hurt, and pain that comes with change. The widower must first grieve his spouse before he can see and appreciate new possibilities."[6]

Susan David, a psychologist at Harvard Medical School and author of *Emotional Agility*, argues that workplaces focus on positivity to the detriment of well-being, and that the suppression of negative emotions can be harmful. "Teams that feel safe enough to articulate discontent or talk about frustration are the most high-functioning teams," she notes. "When we only allow some emotions, we create a huge amount of emotional labor. We also create a situation for individuals that is psychologically unhealthy and undermines the organization's ability to learn and function more effectively."[7] It only makes sense that if people are busy suppressing some parts of their thoughts and emotions, they won't be able to participate or focus fully.

Philanthropy has a culture of politeness. On the surface, everyone gets along and seems happy to work together, but there are often simmering issues that cannot be addressed because it is taboo to "rock the boat." Pushing back is frowned upon. Being nice isn't a problem per se, but when people cannot speak their minds or address what concerns them, we may miss out on the best thinking, and feelings of bitterness can begin to fester.

The role for leaders is to create a safe space for vulnerability by sharing their own trauma and grief, and modeling listening, compassion, and empathy. These developments are part of the shift toward enabling people to bring their full selves to work. Grieving needs to happen on an individual level and also within all the institutions along the loans-to-gifts spectrum.

STEP TWO

Apologize

Apologizing turns us from the inward focus of grief, outward to the Others who were harmed. Around money, apologies are due for where the wealth came from—almost always from the theft of land and resources, the exploitation of slaves and low-wage workers. Apologies are due for how that wealth was maneuvered out of appropriate taxation—off shore, into havens, into foundations—and shirked its responsibility in paying for roads, bridges, public schools, firefighters, eldercare, etc. Apologies are due for the majority of investments, which support harmful industries, practices, and regimes. Apologies are due for the greed and pettiness that characterize a lot of our everyday behavior and interactions around money, all of which arise out of the separation paradigm, the myth of scarcity, this idea that we're not together in this thing called life.

Apologizing requires that white people of wealth snap out of their paralyzing white fragility and guilt, and just step up. It requires that people of color and Indigenous people dismantle their internalized oppression and admit that they too were infected by the colonizer virus. Basically, it requires everyone to grow up and take responsibility for their actions, in order to move forward.

Pumla Gobodo-Madikizela is a South African psychologist and academic who participated in the South African Truth and Reconciliation Committee (TRC). The TRC was a restorative justice process between victims and perpetrators of apartheid-era violence in South Africa. In her book *A Human Being Died that Night*, she beautifully describes the experiences of a society coming to terms with its past:

> A genuine apology focuses on the feelings of the other rather than on how the one who is apologizing is going to benefit in the end. It seeks to acknowledge full responsibility for an act, and does not use self-serving language to justify the behavior of the person asking forgiveness. A sincere apology does not seek to erase what was done. No amount of words can undo past wrongs. Nothing can ever reverse injustices committed against others. But an apology pronounced in the context of horrible acts has the potential for transformation. It clears or "settles" the air in order to begin reconstructing the broken connections between two human beings.[1]

Decent people and decent societies admit when they've done wrong. There are places in the world that have made a good faith effort at acknowledging their mistakes and at least beginning the process of apologizing: South Africa post-apartheid and Germany after World War II come to mind.

In 2008, in front of Parliament, the Prime Minister of Australia Kevin Rudd issued a formal apology to Aborigines for federal policies that "inflicted profound grief, suffering, and loss on these our fellow Australians."[2] Canada is another place, like South Africa, where a

Truth and Reconciliation process has taken place, in Canada's case around the experiences of Native peoples. In 2006, Canada launched a Truth and Reconciliation Commission after the closing of the last of their Indian boarding schools in 1996, which had removed some 150,000 Native children from their families. In the worst cases, students died. Many others experienced psychological, physical, and sexual abuse.[3]

In the United States, an official apology for slavery from Congress took until June 2009, during President Obama's first term. In December of the same year, with little fanfare, Obama signed off on the historic Native American Apology Resolution as part of a defense appropriations spending bill, apologizing "on behalf of the people of the United States to all Native peoples for the many instances of violence, maltreatment, and neglect inflicted on Native peoples by citizens of the United States." The resolution also included a disclaimer: Nothing in it authorizes or supports any legal claims against the United States.[4] (Cue the music for *Sorry Not Sorry* by Demi Lovato.)

Native critics said that the lack of publicity around the announcement lessened its impact as an official apology. "What kind of an apology is it when they don't tell the people they are apologizing to?" asked Robert J. Coulter, executive director of the Indian Law Center. "For an apology to have any meaning at all, you do have to tell the people you're apologizing to."[5] But at least it was a start.

Then there are places that stubbornly refuse to apologize. In *The Empire Pays Back*, a British documentary that first aired in 2005, the director Robert Beckford called out the British. He posed the questions: Why has Britain made no apology for African slavery? Why was there no public monument in London on the scale of Berlin's Holocaust Memorial and Museum? Why was there no recognition of how the prosperity of modern Britain was made possible by wealth extracted from Africa and Africans?[6] Given Prime Minister Tony Blair's 1997 apology to the Irish for England's role in the potato famine, it should be a source of enormous embarrassment that the country has never apologized for its activities in any of its former colonies, Africa most of all. Instead there is widespread ambivalence today among British citizens about whether or not colonization was a good thing. #sorrynotsorry

~~~

As Peter Buffett has written, "I believe that words can change the world. On a personal level, when we say, 'I hear you' or 'I'm sorry,' worlds can change."[7]

After investigating her ancestry and discovering her own family's involvement in land theft and slavery, Hilary Giovale of the Geo Family Foundation wrote a letter acknowledging these truths and sent it to 15 of her friends, including people of color, Indigenous people, and white people. "It was very, very scary, because that's not something we talk about in America. But amazingly, I was shown a great deal of compassion. It was a beautiful process."

In becoming transparent about her ancestry, Hilary says, "My heart was calling me to apologize, but for some time, I still felt ambivalent about it. I was worried that any apology I could give would seem insincere, insufficient, or that it would generate fresh pain and inflict further harm." However, through ensuing conversations, collaborative relationships, and decolonization work, she eventually found the strength to apologize. This is the apology she works with today:

> *To my Indigenous Relatives and Relatives of Color: I apologize for my ignorance of the harm that came to you and the horrors you survived through many generations. I apologize for my unconscious racism and white supremacy, and the pain they have caused you. I apologize for the silent ways I gave my own comfort priority over your existence as a sovereign human being. When I dishonored you, I dishonored my own humanity and the humanity of all our children. I am sorry. I love you. Please forgive me.*

> *To my European-Descended Relatives: I apologize for all the times I have judged you instead of allowing myself to feel the grief of our collective spiritual impoverishment and cultural amnesia. I apologize for seeing you as a monster of oppression, instead of a Child of Creation. I apologize for disassociating from you and denying that we are related. When I judged you, I judged my own ancestors, my children, and myself. I am sorry. I love you. Please forgive me.[8]*

She shakes her head at the fact that it took her until adulthood—and it took her family nine generations of colonization—before this moment occurred in which she finally found the courage to apologize. Yet as the civil rights activist W. E. B. Du Bois said, "It is *never* too late to mend. Nothing is so bad that good may not be put into it and make it better and save it from utter loss."[9]

Not long ago I was at a funders meeting in Charleston, South Carolina, where a network called Grant Makers for Southern Progress gathered and released a new report about funding in the South. A young white man got up to present this report. His first slide was an image of a historic census document from his great-grandfather that listed all the slaves he owned and their names. "I feel like people should know where I come from," the young man said, "and I'm sorry that this is where I come from, but I want to be a part of changing things." There we were in a plantation-style hotel, just blocks from where slaves were actually sold. It had to be terrifying for him to stand up in front of so many Black faces in his audience and say what he said. But it felt as if his action brought the room together. Sure enough, later that night I was in a car full of Black folks who had been at the presentation. They said how moved they were, and how they loved that young white man. Not recognizing history is very painful for a lot of people.

I also spoke to Sarah Lyons, one of the cofounders of a Canadian nonprofit called the Circle on Philanthropy and Aboriginal People in Canada, or the Circle, for short. Its mission is to foster more and better conversations, connections, and relationships among Aboriginal peoples and philanthropic organizations. The Circle is urging Canada's philanthropy community to further the work of the Truth and Reconciliation Commission, which officially ended in 2015, and demonstrate ongoing leadership on reconciliation and healing.

Sarah told me: "The level of awareness and interest in the notion of reconciliation is really high, and foundations are really, I think genuinely, both committed to being part of change, and interested in figuring out and working with others in what their piece of that is." One of their initiatives has involved getting foundations to sign a "Declaration of Action" that commits the undersigned foundations to "Learn and Remember" about the tragedy that was the Indian Residential School System experience; to "Understand and Acknowledge" by "recognizing the need for an ongoing commitment to support the continuation of this multi-generational journey of healing and reconciliation;" and to "Participate and Act" by "sharing our networks, our voices, and our resources to include and benefit Aboriginal peoples."[10] As Sarah put it, foundations who sign it are saying "we're aware there's an unacceptable situation in terms of quality of life and political representation of Indigenous peoples, and we commit to being part of the change."[11]

In the United States and in other nations, the philanthropic community and the financial community, especially those in social finance, could adopt a declaration just like this, and even spearhead the creation of Truth and Reconciliation Committees. I would love to hear funders acknowledge the reality of the situation around wealth, to say, "This is not our money. This wealth was created on the backs of Native people, whose role was never compensated and never acknowledged. This wealth was made on the backs of enslaved Africans. This wealth was made with stolen resources on stolen land with slave labor or low-wage labor. This wealth was stolen again when it was shielded from taxation, which would have generated revenue to pay for community improvements and programs. We acknowledge that, and we apologize. We're sorry."

Just to hear that would mean the world.

I want to be clear: Just because you apologize for bad behavior does not mean you are entitled to forgiveness or reconciliation. That's a whole other part of the process, but apologizing is a necessary step before either can happen.

STEP THREE

Listen

66 **I**f you want to learn, you have to give up talking," Jennifer Buffett of the NoVo Foundation told me in our conversations. Her husband, Peter, added: "I've had this wonderful, privileged, lucky life in so many ways, so I shouldn't be the one saying, 'Here's how to solve the problem.' The people who are experiencing it should say that. What you need to do is get really humble, and listen, and learn. . . . Transformational change will always require challenging conversations about 'us'— not a monologue about helping 'them.'"[1]

If I had a dollar for every time someone told me that the folks holding the purse strings don't really listen! After 15 years in the field of philanthropy, I can't believe I'm still hearing this. Every human deserves the dignity of being heard. The lack of listening extends far beyond philanthropy and the finance sector, of course. You could argue that the deep political divisions in the United States are caused by and worsened by a refusal from both sides to listen to each other and engage in civil conversation. People need to be reminded what it means to listen and be able to disagree without immediately devolving to hate and demonization. While funders should be devoting resources to supporting these kinds of respectful conversations happening, first off, funders themselves have to practice better listening.

Why is it so difficult for people and institutions of wealth to listen? They believe that they know more than others and know what's best for others. They're not open to learning or being influenced. They make positive assumptions about their own abilities and negative assumptions about everyone else. This is a reflection of the power dynamic, the white savior mentality. It's about a lack of humility and a desire to be in control.

Jed Emerson, the "godfather of impact investing," says that funders are plagued by "'mansplaining,' where men, regardless of whether or not they know anything about the topic, they just go into this explanation. As a field, we suffer from that, because you've got entrepreneurs who are looking for capital, and God forbid they don't have the right answer when they're talking to a potential investor! . . . There's a tendency to want to always be right, to want to always have the answer, to want to always convince others of your righteousness. Those elements make for bad investing. They may make for good short-term investing, but they don't make for good long-term value creation beyond simple financial returns."[2]

Even before failing to listen, funders and investors often exert control by framing the conversation and asking only certain kinds of questions. That already places limits on what's possible, what can or cannot be said, not to mention the predominance of advice given by funders, which shuts down conversation automatically. There is rarely space for an honest dialogue about what's really going on, the challenges being faced, because everyone's putting on a happy, successful face for the one holding the purse strings. When funders ignore input from outside their walls, they stifle priceless creativity and leadership.

Organizations evolve in the direction of the questions that funders most persistently and passionately ask. Rather than asking what's wrong, what needs to be fixed, what's broken, what if philanthropy asked a community what it is most proud of and how it could support that? Questions about what is working well are energizing: their answers spread the stories of solutions and the design of those solutions.

Otto Scharmer, a professor of leadership and management at Massachusetts Institute of Technology, says that listening is key to leadership, but not just any kind of listening. He differentiates between "downloading," which is when we only hear things that confirm what we already know; "factual listening," when we filter what we hear in search of new data and evidence; "empathetic listening," which puts us in the shoes of the speaker, connecting and feeling what s/he feels; and finally, "generative listening," in which we enter almost a meditative flow state, which enables us "to connect to the highest future possibility that can emerge."[3] We need to be striving for empathetic listening 100 percent of the time in order to heal the past, and generative listening as often as we can in order to move forward and build new organizations and new culture.

Because wealth tends to have an isolating effect—which is only heightened when ivory towers are situated and built to exclude and alienate the people seeking funding—listening is key to undoing the rigid structures of colonization that keep wealth from flowing. Focused listening allows you to get a glimpse of what it is like to be someone else and see the world through their eyes. Being able to adopt the mindset of a person with a different background than yourself creates openness in you. It will challenge your assumptions and limiting beliefs. It may lead you to solutions or ideas that you would never otherwise have been able to access.

Words are important. In many traditions, there is a belief that words have a power to create reality and must be used with discretion and responsibility. Yet people communicate much more than just the *content* of what they say. People's tone of voice, their use of metaphor, their body language also tell us a lot about their experience, their identity, and their worldview.

So good listening includes being:

- **Open:** not predetermining the appropriate content of communications
- **Empathetic:** truly inviting in and making space for the feelings and wisdom of the speaker
- **Holistic:** including what is said in ways that do not use words

In fact, we could call it "listening in color," a specific way to combat the trauma of global bleaching's relentless destruction of the number of voices that were amplified and heard within the white supremacist, colonial context.

Listening in color is a superpower that you can wield to change the status quo, no matter what role you play inside an institution on the loans-to-gifts spectrum. You may have little influence to impact a board or CEO's funding strategy, but you can always listen to those seeking funding with an open heart. Listening attentively means holding back your own conclusions, opinions, and judgments. You do not need to jump in and say, "Me too!" This just moves the focus away from the other person and back to yourself. Give them room to breathe and take risks in conversation. No monologues and no mansplaining. Replace advice with openness and curiosity.

When funders listen in color, everyone will flourish as a result.

Relate

My favorite book as a child was *How to Win Friends and Influence People* by Dale Carnegie. I've read it dozens of times because I was clear at an early age that whatever I ended doing in life would involve the world's more precious resource: people. We are all in the people business! However, every institution and process dealing with money I've experienced has this in common: they focus on transactions rather than relationships.

To prioritize relationship means that cultivating strong, authentic, caring human connection is valued over and above returns on investments and measurable results. It means recognizing that rather than the cash, relationships are an institution's greatest asset, even for one that is focused on money. It means that those with wealth are not reduced to cash machines and those seeking funding are not reduced to gold diggers. There are real people hiding inside the business suits.

To create an atmosphere in which relationships come first, we need to start with the location and design of the space. No more ivory towers. If it's serious about connecting to the communities it serves, a foundation shouldn't be set off in the woods surrounded by deer, with the offices occupying buildings that resemble plantations and the rooms filled with antiques that look like they belonged to royal families. How can you serve disabled people if your rooms are not accessible to them? How can you serve trans people if your restrooms are not welcoming to them? And why don't the windows open in these places, when the fields of philanthropy and finance so desperately need a breath of fresh air?

Banks and investment firms don't have to feel like they were carved from a block of ice, intimidating with their angular slick surfaces and long rectangular tables with "VIP seating" on either end. Funders' offices don't have to look like yurts, either, but there's compelling evidence that spaces that encourage relationships have rounded edges and warm textiles, with the kitchen central. When people sit in circles they feel like they're on more equal footing with one another. When people can cook and eat together, they connect on a human level. When people are physically comfortable, they are more likely to be themselves.

The influential architect and design theorist Christopher Alexander began critiquing contemporary architecture for creating lifeless, impersonal spaces way back in the mid-1970s, publishing a series of books in which he calls instead for structures that possess a quality of aliveness and wholeness, "beautiful places, places where you feel yourself, places where you feel alive."[1] These qualities impact the social interactions that can happen in those structures. As he writes elsewhere: "The structure of life I have described in buildings— the structure which I believe to be objective—is deeply and inextricably connected with the human person, and with the innermost nature of human feeling."[2] There are literally certain kinds of spaces that make people feel welcome, that make visitors feel on equal footing with those already in the building, that encourage people to interact and relate. Those are decolonized spaces.

"We have this belief that everything is about relationships," Pamela Shifman, the executive director of the NoVo Foundation, told me. "So we actually spend almost no time on the written applications and we try to make things super easy. Often the best work is happening in places where people aren't writing the best applications about the work. That's also really true outside the U.S., like a million percent. We're also trying to have meetings not only at our office but to go to others. These things may seem small, but they create the opportunity for different kinds of conversations and relationships to emerge."[3]

Founded by Peter Buffett and his wife, Jennifer Buffett, NoVo's mission is to "foster a transformation from a world of domination and exploitation to one of collaboration and partnership." Pamela continued:

> It's good for both sides. As funders, we can tell when someone treats you as an ATM machine, just figuring how they're going to get the money out of me and don't see anything about me and who I am. So much shifts when we make space for real relationships. We really get to know each other and go deep. We share on a personal level. When you're with someone, you have to be able to really be with them. And know each other. And love each other. And to have real tension. You have to be able to disagree and even fight, and then say, *It's okay. We're still on the same team.* I feel like we have to find ways to be able to develop meaningful relationships with people so that you actually can talk about what's actually going on and figure out how to move forward together.[4]

It's true that relationships are more complicated than transactions, as Pamela points out. There's a reason why folks vow to stick together *for better or for worse, for richer or for poorer, in sickness and in health*. Real, complex relationships are necessary not only for whatever the present entails but also to face challenges in the future. Relationships create resilience; transactions don't.

Transactions are superficial. It's like the difference between dating and relating in this day and age, where dating apps are like marketplaces, and you create profiles to sell yourself. It's about selling: making yourself attractive to someone else. You're trying to pass a test and at the same time you're judging someone else's presentation to see if they're good enough for you. Relating, on the other hand, is about authenticity and vulnerability. You let yourself be seen for who you are and you accept the other person for who they are. You allow the other person the benefit of the doubt. Mutual trust, respect, and appreciation deepen a relationship. We commit to supporting the success of the other person. We develop a sense that we are in this together.

There's a list of 36 questions developed by a psychologist named Arthur Aron who studies intimacy; it became a viral sensation after appearing in the *New York Times* "Modern Love" column in 2015. The questions are designed to bring two strangers along the path of relationship, breaking down barriers gradually by revealing people's concerns, hopes, dreams, and secrets. Twenty-five questions in, after quite a bit of territory has been covered, each person is asked to make three true "we" statements that refer to the two of them together—in other words, at this point, they're in a relationship. Aron's 36 questions been used in studies to explore cross-race relationships and prejudice; they've been used to reduce tensions between police officers and community members.[5] How great would it be if, alongside asking for your business plan and your unique proposition and your rate of return, funders asked the 36 questions, or at least a selection of them, until both sides could make three true "we" statements?

Jennifer Buffett explained what relationships looks like in the context of NoVo's connection with their grantees: "If you want trust, then you have to give trust and the benefit of the doubt. We give them a commitment of seven years' funding or five years' funding . . . a nice timeline. And we say, you come back to us at the end of the year, and you can be totally honest, you're going to get the money through the whole seven years no matter what. So tell us what you did, what did you find out? What problems emerged? And then give them the second and the third year, and keep asking and keep giving, give it freely with no preconceived mind conditions, or stipulations and no fear. Mistakes will be made. That's okay. Everyone learns."[6] It's about patience and unconditional care and trust.

~~~~

There are a lot of vibrant conversations happening in the field of organizational design that explore what it looks like when an organization is structured horizontally: when the people who used to be powerless, at the bottom of the old pyramid model, are empowered and have a sense of agency. There are a lot of conversations about purpose-driven organizations and workplaces where the whole person is welcome.

Many industries and businesses have begun experimenting with moving toward open, participatory, and transparent processes. They are moving toward seeking and incorporating wisdom from all levels of the organization as well as from users or "the crowd." The functions of decision making, goal setting, creation, implementation, and evaluation are being distributed among all these stakeholders as well, with the recognition that important insights and innovations come from those who were previously not included.

Many are exploring the benefits of sharing power, for example in new forms of cooperative ownership or shareholding. The barriers between designer and consumer, expert and user are dissolving. There is more role fluidity. In the words of Jeremy Heimans, who writes about the distinction between "old power" and "new power": "New power operates differently, like a current. It is made by many; it is open, participatory, and peer-driven. It uploads and it shares. Like water or electricity, it's most forceful when it surges. The goal with new power is not to hoard it but to channel it."[7]

What if funders moved from hoarding resources and operating in obscurity to becoming transparent, accountable, and participatory? Rather than the formality of professionalism, it would rely on the wisdom of the community. Rather than dinosaur-style "command-and-control" methods that are based in scarcity and separation, funders would embrace abundance and trust.

What if the question became "How can everyone be powerful?" rather than "How can everyone have equal power?" In his book on organizational design that adopts a framework of organization-as-organism rather than organization-as-machine, the Belgian scholar of human behavior and management Frederic Laloux writes: "[P]eople can hold different levels of power, and yet everyone can be powerful . . . [as] in an ecosystem, interconnected organisms thrive without one holding power over another . . . the point is not to make everyone equal; it is to allow all employees to grow into the strongest, healthiest version of themselves."[8]

In fact, what if funders no longer assumed that disadvantaged communities and individuals needed to be empowered at all? What if we acknowledged how powerful they inherently are? The irony of a project of empowerment is that it requires victims: if you need someone to give up power and make space for you, then you are a victim of the power dynamic. Transcending the Drama Triangle roles of perpetrator, victim, and savior involves everyone being allocated with agency and responsibility.

We don't see a lot of these human-centered, horizontal, holistic models being adapted in the institutions along the loans-to-gifts spectrum, but there's no reason we can't start.

Represent

Effectively moving money to where the hurt is worst—using money as medicine—requires the funder to have deep, authentic knowledge of the issues and communities that will be putting the funding to use. Deep authentic knowledge does not come from reading some stats, reports, or articles; it doesn't even come from a site visit to that community or interviewing someone from the affected community. It comes from living inside that community and experiencing that issue for oneself. Period.

Daryn Dodson's work through Illumen Capital is based on the psychology of racial biases and how people miss opportunities because of it, applying that to a financial framework. He notes:

> One of the things that was missing in terms of the overall sector of impact investing was the connection of entrepreneurs to the communities which they're trying to transform and create solutions for, or what Bryan Stevenson calls 'proximity.' So the idea that people who are investing large amounts of money to transform the world would sit down with the communities that they're

trying to transform is a really important pillar of
what we're trying to accomplish.[1]

Bryan Stevenson, author of *Just Mercy* and the executive director of the Equal Justice Initiative, explains
"proximity" as "Get close to the things that matter, get
close to the places where there is inequality and suffering, get close to the spaces where people feel oppressed,
burdened, and abused. See what it does to your capacity
to make a difference, see what it does to you."[2]

This should not be a radical idea, people. In some
sectors it's not. For example, in order to receive federal
funds, 51 percent of a federally qualified health center's
board has to be patients, which is to say, representatives
of the people served. Yet among the majority of foundations, there's not a single person on staff—not to speak of
on the board—who possesses that lived experience and
wisdom. Gara LaMarche of the Democracy Alliance told
me, "I think the most fundamental thing that philanthropies can do is democratize themselves, so that the
decision making is made by people the most affected. A
more established way of doing that, which still people
don't do enough, is to have boards that are really reflect-
ing communities."[3]

The good news is: a handful of funders are already
experimenting with collaboration and participation and
representation. The Potlatch Fund in Seattle, created in
2004 with the sole focus of funding Native communities in the Northwest—one of the only foundations in
the country giving 100 percent to Natives—has bylaws
stipulating that two-thirds of the board seats be held by
Native Americans. Their funding priorities are determined by talking circles in Native communities, and
decided there in the talking circles based on consensus.

I spoke to Nevin Öztop from FRIDA, a fund for young feminists in the Global South that employs a participatory grantmaking process. They receive about 1,000 applicants per grantmaking cycle, who are then "invited to comment and vote on the 100 groups that they think should receive funding." The peer-review process promotes movement building in that it enhances critical analysis, connections, solidarity, and accountability between applicants. All of FRIDA's grants are awarded as flexible funds and core support, which allows groups to define their own budgets and dedicate funds where they are most needed. In particular, FRIDA's grants can be used to cover traditionally and increasingly underfunded areas like overhead and general operating costs.

Nevin told me a story of one group who had applied, received one of the highest ratings from their peers, but then stepped back and offered their FRIDA grant to another group whom they felt needed the money more. "I think the reason they did that was because they felt like it was their own money. There was an ownership of resources. They felt like they could decide on the fate of that money. We re-granted it to another group that they thought should receive funding. It was such a nice moment."[4]

One of the NoVo Foundation's newest projects is turning a former women's prison in New York City into a women's building. NoVo's executive director Pamela Shifman told me, "We have a big advisory circle made up of 21 women. Some are formerly incarcerated women; some are women activists. Some will be potential tenants themselves, but they're also on the selection committee for tenants."[5] This is what empowered representation looks like.

Another potent example comes from the Brooklyn Community Foundation, which launched an initiative called Neighborhood Strength in the Crown Heights neighborhood in 2014. Neighborhood Strength positions the residents of the neighborhood as the key decision makers for the foundation's investments. The foundation brought together more than 130 residents in three sessions in the fall of 2016 to identify their top concerns for the neighborhood and propose solutions. Then 17 highly engaged residents came together to form an advisory council that reviewed those concerns and agreed on a focus, their one big idea: public space. The foundation set the terms of a request-for-proposals process based on the advisory council's recommendation. When the proposals came in, the advisory council selected the winning projects.[6]

These are all great steps forward toward real representation from some of the most progressive funders out there. A participatory model has also been attempted in municipalities around the world and was even experimented with by the White House: it's called participatory budgeting. In Porto Alegre, Brazil, where the idea was born some 25 years ago, as many as 50,000 residents vote on how to spend public money each year. New York and Boston have experimented with it. And under the Obama administration, participatory budgeting became an option for determining how to spend community development block-grant money from the Department of Housing and Urban Development.[7]

Granted, the model risks reinforcing white privilege and class privilege, since currently more white middle- and upper-class voters vote in participatory budgeting processes, but it doesn't have to be that way. In 2013 in Chicago, one councilman (Moore, of the Forty-Ninth

Ward) took the $1.3 million "menu money" given by the city to each of the city's 50 councilmembers for capital improvements, and opened up the allocation process to his community. People starting at age 16 (younger than with a regular election, and residents, not just citizens) were invited to vote on the menu money.[8] In the case of that Chicago ward, a clear intention and outreach made the process more truly democratic and representative of the population.

~~~

In order for us to decolonize wealth, at least half of the people who make the decisions about where money goes—at least 50 percent of staff, 50 percent of advisors, 50 percent of board members—should have intimate, authentic knowledge of the issues and communities involved. This means that some of the usual suspects, the white saviors, will have to give up their seats. They'll have to step back, rather than just make a token seat open next to them. This will definitely require an attitude adjustment for some. As Jordan Flaherty writes in his book on the savior complex: "For people born into privilege, decentering yourself can feel difficult. It involves giving up a certain amount of privilege. . . ."[9] And as the saying goes, *when you're accustomed to privilege, equality feels like oppression.* That discomfort is part of the healing.

As Paulina Helm Hernandez, a queer Latina organizer and artist, former codirector of Southerners On New Ground (SONG), and now a program officer at the Foundation for a Just Society, said to white people wanting to be allies to people of color: "You don't have to always be the final vote on the strategy, pace, timing, tone and approach. Put another way, it means you have to learn how to share political imagination, power, and work without having to always be in charge. . . . You have to be willing to trust leaders of color who have the track record, integrity, and vision to get things done."[10]

In 2017, for the first time in its history, the Andrus Family Fund (AFF) invited three community board members to join its board of directors, including yours truly. We are fully fledged trustees, with the same rights and votes as the family board members. Having never previously included non-family members on the board, when they decided to open seats to the community, rather than starting with a single token seat, they opened up three seats simultaneously. There's some research that when integrating new people into an existing culture or structure, you want to shoot for the newbies being 30 percent of the total, or, at a minimum, three people.[11]

AFF's strategy reflected their commitment to the foundation authentically representing what will soon be the new American majority. Inviting community board members to join was a natural extension of AFF's social justice values, yet getting to this place of shared power required more than eight years of deep discussion and deliberation to make the jump. Family members on the board revealed to me that the biggest obstacle was their fear of being judged: that it was only because they were family that they were on the board in the first place.

What if foundations had to apply for the honor of funding communities and projects, rather than the other way around? Phillip Jackson, founder of the Black Star Project, has been working to improve the lives of Black Chicagoans for decades. He intentionally built the orga-nization—which provides mentoring, tutoring, parental engagement, politics exposure, career development, violence prevention—with a business model with multiple funding streams, only minimally supported by foundations. This has meant, as Phillip puts it:

> We're able to hold people more accountable who other people dare not hold accountable. . . . Most not-for-profits have a subservient relationship with foundations. That's not something we were willing to be. When we were coming to the foundation, we were saying, "Hey, you need us as much as we need you." That's not something the foundations were used to hearing, but that was our attitude. Our attitude was, look, there are problems out there. These problems need solutions. We have solutions, you have dollars to fund the solutions, let's work together.[12]

Those who are truly intentional about the work of healing from decolonization understand that representation of people of color alone is not sufficient—the outcome is simply token diversity. We must go beyond representation to sharing ownership and full inclusion.

STEP SIX

Invest

When people learn that the same company that is selling a cure is simultaneously contributing to the cause of the disease, they get mad, and understandably so. There was a huge uproar around 2002 when activists revealed this was exactly what was happening with the pink ribbon breast cancer fundraising campaign. Cosmetics companies that were simultaneously using breast-cancer-linked chemicals in their products were "pinkwashing"—enticing consumers with the assurance that they were contributing a portion of their proceeds to fight the disease. I'm sorry to say that this dynamic is taking place in the very heart of philanthropy and ethical investing. And it needs to stop.

Since 1969, U.S. tax law has mandated that foundations pay out a *minimum* of 5 percent of their total assets each year in the form of grants or eligible administration expenses. The "payout rule" was created to prevent foundations from receiving assets but never actually making charitable distributions with them. The other 95 percent of the assets are invested with the goal of earning financial returns that sustain the grantmaking power of the foundation over time. It makes zero sense that a foundation that aims to stop global warming with the

5 percent it pays out would simultaneously invest its
assets in fossil fuel industries, right? Yet this kind of contradiction occurs all the time. This is unconscionable.

What about the 95 percent?! is a question all of us
need to be asking, and almost no one is. It's only just in
recent years, after a decade in the field, that I've awak-
ened to the 95 percent. What is going on with that
money? For those of us in the field, it's as if there's a
firewall. We're kept in the dark about what's happening
on the other side. We're not privy to conversations about
the corpus, yet that's where the real power is, because it's
where the vast, vast majority of the money is working.
The 5 percent we're in charge of allocating is just a drop
in the bucket.

At one of the foundations I worked at, we would
have a quarterly ice cream party to celebrate when our
investments paid off, increasing our corpus. This puzzled
me—*weren't higher levels of giving what we were supposed
to be celebrating?* During my interview with Dana Arviso,
executive director of the Potlatch Fund, we spoke about
the backwardness of the priorities. I began, "In philanthropy we ask how big you are, which foundation has
the largest amount of assets in the bank—"

Dana jumped in, finishing my thought: "That's
where your prestige and your status comes from, rather
than how much you give away."

The Potlatch Fund is named for the potlatch ceremo-
nies common among the tribes of the Pacific Northwest,
who had such an abundance of natural resources that
they began a practice of ceremonially giving it all away—
redistributing wealth. "The status of certain chiefs here
in the Northwest was measured by how many potlatches
they had in their lifetime," Dana told me. "Some of the
most esteemed chiefs in the Northwest had six or seven

potlatches in their lifetime. We're talking about gathering up everything that they had and giving it all away, for the purpose of creating strong relationships with neighboring tribal communities."[1]

Most foundations don't even disclose information about their investments. Of the 10 largest foundations in the United States, only two—the MacArthur Foundation and the W. K. Kellogg Foundation—publish investment returns on their websites.

Meanwhile investors who tout the "doing well by doing good" mantra—whether they call it ethical investing, socially responsible investing, impact investing, even micro-lending—are all too often playing the same game. A portion of their investments may be going to fund solar-powered lamps and clean cookstoves for poor Africans, but meanwhile the majority of their money is "safely" invested in traditional places where a solid return is expected, and that might well mean in mining companies that are destroying the soil and groundwater of those same poor Africans.

It's true that divestment campaigns have been fairly effective at shining the light on these kinds of hypocrisies and inconsistencies with specific issues, most famously with the apartheid regime in South Africa in the 1980s, over the past decade with fossil fuels, and most recently with divestment from banks that supported the Dakota Access Pipeline. The opposite of investment, divestment campaigns put pressure on investors to get rid of stocks, bonds, or investment funds that are supporting that unhealthy, unethical, or downright evil activity. Divestment activists have successfully demanded that municipalities, universities and colleges, religious organizations, retirement funds, and other institutions stop funding the bad stuff. As we saw with the South African divestment campaign, it can really work. By the mid-1980s, 22 countries, 90 cities, and 155 campuses had pulled their funding from companies that did business in South Africa, which contributed to the end of the apartheid government.[2]

But why should philanthropy and ethical investment have to rely on whistleblowers and independent activists to keep the bulk of their assets from causing harm? Not only should those assets be transparent, they should be 100 percent aligned with the mission of the foundation. This is known as mission-related investing. The concept has already found support among many of the big players in philanthropy, including the Kellogg Foundation, the John D. and Catherine T. MacArthur Foundation, the Bill and Melinda Gates Foundation, and Open Society Foundations. In April 2017, the president of the Ford Foundation, Darren Walker, announced that Ford was embracing it as well:

> I am pleased that after many months of analysis and planning, the Ford Foundation's Board of Trustees has authorized the allocation of up to $1 billion of our endowment, to be phased in over 10 years, for mission-related investments. Since the 1980s, divestment movements around the world have asked institutional investors, in particular, to consider how their investments are related to the wider world. Whether they were demanding divestment from tobacco, fossil fuels, or apartheid South Africa, these movements reminded us that our investments are part of a broad ecosystem of consequences, intended and unintended—consequences that we realized we could not ignore. Today, we have an opportunity

to build on this proud, powerful legacy. Previous divestment movements tried to prevent investors from harming society; now, institutional investors can begin to move from "do no harm" to exploring how to "do more good."[3]

The move received a lot of positive attention and will likely inspire other foundations to follow suit, which is definitely positive, but here's the thing: Ford's total endowment is more than $12 billion. So this move doesn't even impact 10 percent of their assets. Darren Walker acknowledged it's just the start; it's not enough to move the dial.

We need to move the dial, people. The F. B. Heron Foundation provides an excellent model to follow. Founded in 1992 with the mission of helping people and communities to move out of poverty and thrive, by 1996 the board began considering what could be done with the 95 percent, realizing that a "foundation should be more than a private investment company that uses its excess cash flow for charitable purposes."[4] Within a decade, Heron's mission-related activity had grown to comprise approximately 40 percent of its overall endowment and included everything from taxable municipal bonds to private equity. In 2012, they decided to go from 40 percent to 100 percent mission-related investments. However, they quickly discovered that there were relatively few truly mission-aligned, poverty-oriented investment managers out there in the market. Instead there were a growing number of impact-screened vehicles. By December 21, 2016, Heron moved the last unscreened piece of its corpus to impact-screened exchange-traded funds (ETFs); up next, they'll be pushing their portfolio from screened-for-impact to invested-for-mission.[5]

And what about risks and returns? Ford's relatively cautious $1 billion over 10 years reflects a fear of "underperformance," as they say in finance language, meaning there's a lower rate of profit. This is sacrilege to many investment committees of foundations, who insist on protecting the endowment for perpetuity. Heron's investment policy statement makes their stance clear:

> For Heron, return is measured both in financial terms and by the degree to which any given use of capital leads to outcomes that are consistent with our philanthropic mission and public purpose. In this policy statement, "risk" refers to the probability of non-performance on both social and financial dimensions, and on the interaction between the two. . . . We believe that investments in targeted enterprises with positive net contribution will perpetuate a cycle of favorable social performance, financial performance, and ultimately financial return.[6]

There are also those who say that the widespread fear of diminished financial returns is bogus. Kristin Hull, an impact investor and advisor based in the San Francisco Bay Area, decided to go 100 percent mission-invested back in 2007, when she moved all the assets of her family foundation out of the market and into seven local community banks. By 2008, when the recession hit, foundation endowments nationwide were down by 28 percent, but her family's was up by 2 percent.[7] Since then her investment philosophy has gotten even sharper: "I just can't invest in any more white men unless they're part of a diverse team. They're already getting the money. Knowing that women receive less that 4 percent of venture capital and people of color just 1 percent, that is the most meaningful and impactful place for me to invest."[8]

Kristin's women-and-people-of-color-only screen for investments is the necessary next step for all of us. It's not enough to just not allow the bulk of our assets to fund the bad stuff, we have to take those assets and invest in the more beautiful world our hearts know is possible. If you believe, as I do, that the best solutions to the current economic and social problems are coming from the very people who were disempowered by the colonial command-and-control, dominate-and-exploit system, then those are the people in whom we need to invest.

My colleague Vanessa Daniel, executive director of the Groundswell Fund, has written that philanthropy's efforts will have gone far enough in this direction "when the majority of foundations acknowledge the fact that white supremacy is in fact blocking progress on everything their trustees care about, and that they have little hope of advancing their missions, whether finding cures for cancer, ending malaria, improving STEM education, promoting the arts, or protecting fragile ecosystems, if they don't fund work that recognizes and dismantles white supremacy."[9]

So, to repeat: there needs to be total transparency around where our assets are invested and those assets must be 100 percent mission-aligned, meaning not just do-no-harm but invested in decolonization, in order to heal divides and restore balance.

Repair

Collectively America's foundations have more than $800 billion in assets. PwC anticipates that global Assets under Management (AuM) will almost double in size by 2025, from $84.9 trillion in 2016 to $111.2 trillion by 2020, and then again to $145.4 trillion by 2025.[1] That's a lot of wealth, and it is wealth that was made on the backs of Natives and African Americans and low-wage workers, following the directives of colonization: *divide, control, and exploit.* Our peoples and our lands were exploited, over generations, over centuries, and ongoing.

Yet despite our role in creating that wealth, white supremacy continues to deny us access to it. We are demeaned for our lack of resources and called lazy. We must jump through hoops and prove ourselves worthy to get a piece of it in the form of loans or grants. As I've shown, of the fairly insignificant 5 percent that is annu-. ally paid out of those $800 billion held by foundations, the little bit of funding specifically earmarked to support people of color has actually been shrinking.[2]

Phillip Jackson from the Black Star Project in Chicago had some stern words for foundations: "These guys will lean back in their ivory towers, in their luxury corporate suites while the blood of Black children is running in the streets of Chicago. I told them, 'You guys are something! You're funding classical music, you're funding impressionistic art . . . and Black children are dying right down the street from where you are.'" He analyzed the grant-making of the MacArthur Foundation, the largest funder in Chicago. "They have $7 billion in assets, and follow the 5 percent payout rule. Out of the $57 million that they give in Chicago, by their own records—I used their own information from their website—only $341,000 went to Black-led, Black-serving organizations."[3] Jackson led a "one-man crusade" to make MacArthur pay attention to the community where it was based, and his courage is commendable, but we shouldn't have to count on community members being so fearless. The commitment to repair should come from the side with the wealth and the power it confers.

As I've noted, loans, venture capital, municipal bonds, and other investments are also smaller in size, harder to get, and often are of poorer quality or higher risk when they go to people of color. And despite the evolution of ethical finance or impact finance, just one of every five dollars under professional financial management is invested following socially ethical strategies,[4] which is likewise no guarantee that people of color will gain access to it.

Since the wealth was extracted from our resources and our work, it is understandable that we're a little frustrated and impatient with institutions of wealth that evaluate our worthiness and risk potential as recipients and then give crumbs.

Reparations are due.

Using money as medicine in its most powerful, direct form means we use it to heal the racial wealth gap.

Decolonizing wealth is, at its essence, about closing
racial wealth gap. Poverty is the product of public policy
and theft, facilitated by white supremacy.

There's an important distinction being made in the
new conversations about reparations—we're not just
talking about making up for the crimes of the past, for the
near genocide of Native Americans 500 to 200 years ago
when the settlers first arrived and spread over the land,
or for the slave trade and slavery. We're talking about
layers and layers of trauma caused by white supremacist exploitation. We're talking about Jim Crow. We're
talking about the exclusions built into the New Deal that
disadvantaged people of color by not counting certain
professions worthy of benefits (such as farmworkers and
domestic workers). We're talking about white boarding
schools that ripped Native American families apart and
stamped out the surviving culture less than a hundred
years ago under the motto "Kill the Indian, Save the
Man." We're talking about how the benefits of the G.I.
Bill were racialized. We're talking about redlining practices. We're talking about the elite universities of this
country being built with profits from slavery and how
students and faculty of color still feel excluded today.
We're talking about the criminal justice system's hugely
disproportionate impact on communities of color. We're
talking about Native Americans' unemployment rates
being 10 times the national average. We're talking about
immigration policies dividing parents from their children right now. We're talking about the violence and
exploitation that have impacted four out of five Native
women. We're talking about the images in the media
that constantly criminalize people of color. We're talking
about the lack of police accountability for the killing
of unarmed Native and Black men and women. We're

talking about the inequality in bank loans and venture capital that impact people of color. Above all, we're talking about how all these—and many other events and policies and cultural practices—have worked together to keep wealth and well-being disproportionately concentrated in white communities.

As Richard F. America of Georgetown University has said, "We want to correct a current, not a past, injustice. The current injustice is that the top 30 percent of the income distribution, overwhelmingly White, enjoys this $5 to $10 trillion unjust enrichment."[5] The writer Ta-Nehisi Coates has also written eloquently on the subject of reparations:

> The wealth gap merely puts a number on something we feel but cannot say—that American prosperity was ill-gotten and selective in its distribution. What is needed is an airing of family secrets, a settling with old ghosts. What is needed is a healing of the American psyche and the banishment of white guilt. What I'm talking about is more than recompense for past injustices—more than a handout, a payoff, hush money, or a reluctant bribe. What I'm talking about is a national reckoning that would lead to spiritual renewal.[6]

So what could the institutions along the loans-to-gifts spectrum do to make and support reparations, in concrete terms?

Philanthropy, as the sector most ostensibly responsible for healing, could and should lead the way. The institutions of philanthropy as a whole could take 10 percent of their assets—10 percent tithed from each foundation in existence—and establish a trust fund to which Native Americans and African Americans could apply for grants for various asset-building projects, such as home ownership, further education, or startup funds for businesses. This reparations tithing among foundations could happen right now, without legislation, as a demonstration of commitment from the philanthropic community. No specifications around how that money is spent, no reporting. No strings attached. Right now.

What if traditional funding mechanisms were replaced by the living resource system approach outlined by my colleagues at Movement Net Lab?

> A living resource system provides a relationship-based approach to resources: resources are identified, linked, moved, supported, and restructured by everyone in the network so that they fit the dynamic nature of networked movements. Resources need to be placed in funding pools where activists can be central to the decision-making process, and funds need to be structured so they can flow to the emerging landscape of self-organized actions rather than just through formal, pre-existing organizations. . . . Funders can have much greater impact if they know how to support with greater precision at each moment, shifting and adapting in real time as the moment evolves. . . .[7]

As early examples of the model, they mention Occupy Sandy—where folks set up Amazon wedding registries that identified needed items that supporters anywhere on earth could purchase to be delivered directly to sites hit by the hurricane—and the Accomplices on Demand network, non-Black people in the Boston area who support Black people's dignity by making their resources, skills, and rolodexes available, and by engaging with people who look like them in antiracist conversations.

Philanthropy and social and ethical finance could also lead the charge in establishing the foundation for what Professor William A. Darity, Jr., of Duke University has called the "Baby Bonds proposal"—although he's actually not talking about a bond; it's more like a trust fund. It would be a publicly provided trust fund given to each newborn child, but the amount of the fund would vary based on the wealth of the child's family. Bill Gates's baby might get $50, Darity has suggested, while the baby of the lowest-income family might get something in the thousands or tens of thousands. This would involve no race-based or heritage-based eligibility but would obviously address the wealth gap for the upcoming and future generations.[8]

A true commitment from the sector of finance to this plan could come in the form of the financial transaction tax (FTT). This miniscule fee charged on the trading of stocks, currencies, debt instruments (like bonds and treasury notes), and derivatives (futures and options) would hardly be felt by investors. An FTT of 0.25 percent—$1 on every $400 of stock traded—would generate hundreds of billions of dollars. Only the top 10 percent of American households own more than $20,000 in stocks directly (directly, as opposed to their pensions, etc., being invested in the market), so it would be this most affluent community for whom the tax of trading activity would even be perceptible. Even with a more conservative rate of tax, such as what was proposed in the Inclusive Prosperity Act introduced in the U.S. House of Representatives in 2012 and the U.S. Senate in 2015 (0.5 percent for all stock transactions, 0.1 percent for all bond transactions, and 0.005 percent on the notional value of all derivative trades), there would still be billion generated per year, according to researchers.[9]

With a handsome sum like $220 billion, we could also look at funding broad social programs like free universal health care or free universal college education, which, as the Movement for Black Lives has suggested, would disproportionately benefit African Americans and could be part of a reparations portfolio. We could also take a chunk of that money and buy land for Natives: land to which we actually have full property rights. (Reservations are held "in trust" by the federal government. The economist Hernando de Soto has called it "dead capital" because we can't put it to use by selling it, buying more to take advantage of economies of scale, or borrowing against it.[10])

In his forthcoming book *From Here to Equality*, coauthored with his wife, Kirsten Mullen, Professor Darity states that a reparations program should accomplish three things in order to provide healing: acknowledgement, restitution, and closure.

> *Acknowledgement* involves the recognition on the part of the beneficiaries of the social injustice that's in question; an acknowledgement on the part of the beneficiaries of that social injustice that there has been a wrong committed and that there must be some form of repair to be provided to the folks who are the victims of that injustice. *Restitution* constitutes the actual program that's enacted to undertake that form of repair. *Closure* constitutes the acknowledgement on the part of the victimized community that they have received a satisfactory act of compensation from the victimizers, and that they have no reason to request anything that's specifically

for their group in the future, unless there's a new wave of injustices.[11]

It's the most powerful commitment that can be made to decolonizing wealth and healing our country. Reparations are the ultimate way to build power in exploited communities. They are the ultimate way to use money as medicine. The institutions of philanthropy and finance can take a giant leap forward and make a commitment, leading the way for government to finally follow suit.

What if foundations, banks, investors, and other institutions controlling wealth could imagine they had no history and no legacy? What if we imagined it was Day One, and our mission is to build the best organization and the best model to achieve everyone's well-being? What if we could be unencumbered by "the way it's done" and liberated to design ourselves from scratch? What if we could use money as medicine? What if we could liberate money to be used as a tool of love?

Yeah, but what if we could?

Coming Full Circle

Decolonization takes us deep into the serpent's belly to confront the white supremacy, the savior complex, and the internalized oppression that are entrenched in ourselves, our institutions, and our society. Only then can we heal from the trauma of the separation worldview that divided the world into Us vs. Them and led to exploitation, fear, and suffering. As we emerge from that process, we can lay a new social and economic foundation, based on new ways of relating to each other and to our resources. With its focus on connection and belonging, the Indigenous worldview—having persisted against all odds, as Indigenous people have—offers inspiration for the way forward.

~~~

The state motto of my home state of North Carolina is *Esse quam videri*, a Latin phrase meaning "to be, rather than to seem." It was also my mother's motto in childrearing. I can hear her now: "No half stepping! We must be *real* Christians, not just in name." "We must *really* love people, not just do good for how it looks."

167

As it turns out, looking back, the first actual philanthropist I ever knew was my mother, not that she would have ever used that word. After nearly a decade and a half of my working in the field, when asked what I do, she will say "philanthropy," but she still stumbles over the word, and I'd be willing to bet money that she couldn't spell it. Can we agree that words in English made of Greek roots were created so we'd have no idea what doctors are saying? So they can charge lots of money when they diagnose you with *hypergargalesthesia*? Yes, that's a real condition: extreme sensitivity to tickling.

But I use the word because if you go by the Greek roots, philanthropy is about the love (*phil*) of humanity (*anthropos*).

To enable me to have a better life, my mom—a single mother—worked two or three shifts a day for most of my childhood, two of those shifts as a domestic worker, providing nursing assistance, helping sick, frail, and elderly (mostly wealthy) folks. A labor of love. Her first shift was at the DMV, a nine to five. Then she went to work providing care in a nursing home or someone's home for her second shift, and then a third shift at someone's home where, if she was lucky, she could get a few hours of sleep between caretaking, until the shift ended at 7:00 a.m., when she'd come home, change clothes, and start all over again. I'd tag along as often as possible. Many nights I hid in the car until the previous nurse left, then she'd sneak me into the houses where I would play the grand pianos, read in the libraries (this is where I discovered *How to Win Friends and Influence People*), and then get tucked into beds or couches.

On her precious days off, did the poor woman put her feet up and eat bonbons? No, she did outreach for church. She helped start a bus ministry. This involved not just her Sundays but her Saturdays too. Actually, *our* Saturdays, because I went along. If I was lucky, we'd stop at Bojangles and grab a cinnamon biscuit first for sustenance. For years, we spent Saturdays going from neighborhood to neighborhood, knocking on doors, saying some variation of "Hi, I'm Sheila from the neighborhood. We go to this church and we just want to invite you to come attend some time. If you have kids, we have a bus that is more than happy to come by and pick them up for Sunday school."

On Sunday mornings when we went to get them, the bus would pull up and most times I was the person to jump out, run up and knock on the door: "I'm here to pick up Tasha." (Or whoever.) Standing there at the door waiting for the kid to come out, I saw a lot of bad things that made me grateful. Although my mom and I were poor, there were people who were much poorer, more troubled. Kids were pushed to the door looking a mess, unwashed, half dressed. Or I'd get sent in to fetch them—"They're in the back room, go get them"—and I'd have to climb over a man passed out from drink, surrounded by beer cans.

My mom was passionate about getting kids to church, and the bus ministry program grew to 300 children in our small community, 300 children getting bused in to attend our church. For years after, to this day, children, now grown children, come running up and hug my mom, shouting, "Sister Sheila, Sister Sheila! You probably don't remember me, but you used to pick me up on a bus and oh my God, you were so special to me."

Most of those kids were just so hungry for love. They'd be trying to climb into my mom's lap, all of them at the same time. They hung out at our house and became my friends. Our home became a place where kids could come and be. My mother hugged them, she listened to them, she loved them. For a lot of those kids, it was the only little bit of light and love they had in their lives.

Anything my mother ever had, she shared, not just with family or friends, but anybody. If her tomato plants produced more than two tomatoes, she'd be bringing those tomatoes to church or setting out a basket in the front yard with a sign that said "Free Tomatoes." Because of how generous my mom was, I had no idea how poor we really were when I was a child. She has spent her life caring for others, sharing resources, raising money for others, giving up her time.

That is an actual philanthropist right there.

And because of her, I decided to pursue a career in healing work. I came very, very close to being a minister. I got my master's in health care administration at the University of North Carolina at Chapel Hill, and then, at 28, I took my first job at a foundation, where each year I gave away 25 to 30 million dollars to support health care in low-income communities. For a while I felt like the luckiest man on the planet, coming from where I had, earning handsomely for doing what I thought was sacred work of love.

As I started off on the journey, I felt about my work in philanthropy what adrienne maree brown, a facilitator and futurist, writes in her beautiful book *Emergent Strategy*: "When we are engaged in acts of love, we humans are at our best and most resilient. The love in romance that makes us want to be better people, the love of children that makes us change our whole lives to meet their needs, the love of family that makes us drop everything to take care of them, the love of community that

makes us work tirelessly with broken hear
humans' core function is love."[1]

Almost 15 years in the field have shown me that
actual philanthropists—those engaged in acts of love for
humanity, like my mother—are much more prevalent
in the regular population, and only rarely found inside
the field's formal institutions: the foundations. Honestly,
the vast majority of foundations have no right to call
what they do *philanthropy*. The word isn't *egoanthropy*,
expertanthropy, or *ROI-anthropy*. But in the field, instead
of love of humanity, there is a lot of the opposite: ego,
greed, fear, blame, and disrespect.

~~~

"That word philanthropy has been so abused," says
Donna, my philanthropy mentor and fellow Lumbee
Indian. "Organized philanthropy has done a disservice
to philanthropy. When people see the word "philanthropy"they automatically think of dollars. In the organized
filed of philanthropy, philanthropy is something we "do."
For me, it's not that. I'm not *doing* philanthropy, I'm *being*
it. There's a difference between acting as a philanthropist
and being a philanthropist. When you're *being* something, it infuses who you are and your contemplation
into it. You connect with the things that resonate with
your being, and your life is a testament to that. That was
the way I was raised, *to be rather than to seem*, which is
the state motto of North Carolina."[2]

Donna has been my "philanthropy mother" since I
got started in the field. She got involved in philanthropy
a couple decades earlier than I did, and happens to
come from the very same land as my people come from,

Robeson County, North Carolina. Like most Natives, and especially the elders, her answers to theoretical questions are rooted in home and family—literally Indigenous:

> My father, bless his heart, he would be 112 now if he was alive. He passed when he was 70. His way of leadership was quiet and powerful. I didn't know everything he had been involved with until he died. People at the funeral coming up to me saying, "If it wasn't for your father, I wouldn't have a job," you know, Indian teachers and others. That's the philanthropy that I grew up with, that was the giving. We were of course poor as church mice. When he died it was just a little over $3,000 a year that was coming into the house and he raised 10 children on that. As poor as anyone was, we didn't go to bed hungry, we were taken care of. He was disabled from the time I was in second grade, from cancer. He lived decades longer than they predicted he would. At the times when he was sickest we had the most food we ever had because that was the traditional way of the community. There was an infrastructure of giving.
>
> Daddy was my mentor in politics. It wasn't about getting credit, it wasn't about what you did, it was what the outcome was, if it helped somebody. I grew up watching all the local politicians come to our house, and it was a house that didn't have indoor plumbing, still had the front porch, kind of, wood shack kind of thing. But it was built on love and it lasted . . . it's still standing after 65 some years. It was the highly segregated part of the county and yet people of all colors and stripes would come into our

house all the time. That's what he believed in, they believed in, Mamma and Daddy.

He would sit in front of the gas station with his buddy. People would come by and talk to him and he would give his opinion of the election and so forth. Politicians visited because they knew he could turn the election to their favor, sitting out in front of that gas station. I called him "the mayor" after I saw the movie *Do the Right Thing*, because the mayor was the one who sat on the front step and did that. That was Daddy, that's what he did. So that's the cultural context I'm rooted in, when I came to philanthropy.[3]

My own grandfather was the same way. He lived in Hope Mills, North Carolina, at the back of a dirt road that you couldn't even get to if it was raining. When he passed away there were hundreds of people who came to his funeral, whose lives he had touched and I had no idea. I knew he spent a few days each week visiting men in the county jail. I had never known he had become the chaplain for Cumberland County in an official capacity. At his funeral, one after another, people stood and said, "I was in jail, your granddaddy talked to me and changed my life and now I'm doing this, this, and this." I had no idea because he was just my quiet, very quiet, simple grandfather.

Donna nods, hearing about my grandfather. "We are the original philanthropists, Natives," she says. "I mean Indigenous people worldwide. It's so obvious that this is an Indigenous way. It's not a Lumbee way, Navajo way, or a Maori way. It's an Indigenous way that cuts across continents, the original way of being and giving."[4]

This was echoed in my interview with Dana Arviso, the executive director of the Potlatch Fund. She told me the story of a conversation she'd led about poverty reduction strategies among a gathering of Natives in the Cheyenne River territory. "They told me they don't have a word for poverty," she said. "The closest thing that they had as an explanation for poverty was 'to be without family.'" Which is basically unheard of. "They were saying it was a foreign concept to them that someone could be just so isolated and so without any sort of a safety net or a family or a sense of kinship that they would be suffering from poverty," she continued. Dana is Navajo, and we compared notes on the traditions in our respective communities.

"If someone is sick or if someone passes away you will never lack for food. It's just like the food comes out the woodwork. If you're sick there's a system in place to make sure that food and support are coming your way," I told her.

"Absolutely," she agreed. "There's a lot of showing up with food, showing up to help and sit with people in time of mourning. Just showing up. I mean, that's one of the biggest lessons I learned from my family: you may not know what to do, but you better show up. Whether that means sharing food, sharing firewood, sharing whatever you had. Taking in extended family because they're going through a rough time and raising their kids. I think that's the biggest difference I see between kind of this mainstream framework and Native communities is that there's such a focus on individualism. And in our communities it's like, no, we are not a healthy community if we're not taking care of everybody."[5]

We are not a healthy community unless we're taking care of everybody, and I mean all our relations, inside and outside our tribes.

~~~

Philanthropy and charitable acts are often called altruistic. Altruism is about doing things for others, unselfishly, without expectation of reward or acknowledgement, and maybe even at some cost to oneself. In zoology, altruism is a little more extreme. It's usually an action that benefits the rest of the species at the actual expense of the individual, like an ant who allows her sisters and brothers to use her body as a bridge across water and then drowns. In human behavior it's meant less literally—there's no expectation that a donor is dying for the cause—still, there's an aspect of self-sacrifice. Many people hold this kind of self-sacrifice for others as the highest form of generosity and kindness.

Yet . . . how often is it called *altruism* when sacrifices are made by people from whom we assume and expect selflessness? We don't call it altruism when a mother stays awake all night by her child's bedside. We don't even call it altruism when a home care worker stays way beyond overtime, until the hurricane has blown over, to ensure the safety of her elderly charge. We *expect* certain kinds of people to make sacrifices. Apparently we reserve the term *altruism* for the privileged, fortunate, entitled people for whom self-sacrifice is a stretch, is unexpected.

The anthropologist David Graeber notes that small societies without money or markets (like Indigenous tribes in the Amazon basin or Papua New Guinea) don't even possess words in their vocabularies for either "altruism" or "self-interest." Those two extremes oversimplify the reason for human interactions around giving, sharing, and hoarding resources, he says, which are always reflective of much more complicated motivations, including solidarity, pride, desire, envy, the anticipation of shared enjoyment, etc. It's the entire web of our relationships that are at the core of our generosity.[6]

When you look more closely, altruism is actually a fundamental reflection of the separation paradigm, the Us vs. Them mindset. Linguistically it's literally about Other-ing—the word comes from the Latin root *alter*, "other." Altruism also is a linear concept: it moves in one direction, from the Have to the Have Not, a one-way flow of resources. Altruism is the poster child for white saviors.

The Native worldview shifts the focus from altruism to reciprocity. Reciprocity is based on our fundamental interconnection—there is no Other, no Us vs. Them, no Haves vs. Have Nots. Reciprocity is the sense that I'm going to give to you because I know you would do the same for me. No one is just a giver or just a taker; we're all both at some point in our lives. This also reflects a cyclical dynamic, as opposed to a one-off, one-way relationship. The Native botanist Robin Wall Kimmerer writes in her book *Braiding Sweetgrass*, "Reciprocity is a matter of keeping the gift in motion through self-perpetuating cycles of giving and receiving. . . . Through reciprocity the gift is replenished. All of our flourishing is mutual."[7]

The Native principle of reciprocity is where the white colonizers and settlers got the concept of "Indian giver." Natives expressed that any gift was given within the expectation of an ongoing relationship, the idea that I give you this because I know you would (and will, at some point) do the same for me. Mutual dependence is necessary for social well-being. We are symbiotic. All of our flourishing is mutual. The white people got all holier-than-thou about it, how a gift isn't actually a gift unless there's no expectation of return. But the cyclical nature of reciprocity is actually the truth of things. As the cultural scholar Lewis Hyde describes in his book *The Gift*, the very essence of a gift, as contrasted with a commodity, is its *relational* quality. Gifts aren't actually "free" even when they don't cost anything. There are always strings attached: a gift is always tied to a relationship.

The supposed selflessness of pure altruism doesn't exist. There's really no such thing as the self completely disconnected from what's outside the self, the Other. What's truer to the way things really are—interconnected and interdependent—is reciprocity. Reciprocity means we are only a healthy community if we're taking care of everybody.

~~~

In 2016, Natives received a lot of positive media coverage and solidarity around the Standing Rock protests. In the spring of 2016, a call went out on the Standing Rock Sioux Indian Reservation to stop the proposed 1,172-mile Dakota Access Pipeline. Standing Rock sits on the border of North and South Dakota, and the pipeline threatens not only the reservation's vital water source, sacred lands, and ancestral burial grounds, but also the aquifer of the Missouri River that provides drinking water to 10 million Americans.[8] The call was answered—and echoed—by thousands of people across the United States and beyond, from both Native and orphan peoples.

Standing Rock was a historic moment, a gathering of tribes that hadn't been seen in over 100 years. I want to underscore this. Native Americans are not one lump of homogenous people. We differ starkly in our ways, and we're often at odds with each other. We sometimes compete with each other for federal support or fishing rights. In the end, we're soaking in the same colonized atmosphere as the rest of the country (and globe), and we're infected by the colonizer virus and internalized oppression just like other communities are. So the fact that all the tribes put aside their differences and came together to support the Sioux over the contested black snake of a pipeline was a big deal.

Standing Rock—a camp of 4,000 to 5,000 people strong at its height—was managed by a distributed leadership structure involving elders, women, and youth, using community assembly meetings and technology to organize. Photographer Camille Seaman of the Shinnecock Nation reflected on her time at the encampment:

> Before dawn every day, a rider on horseback (or, sometimes, a driver in a car) would make their way through camp, saying, "Good morning, my relatives! It's a beautiful day. Wake up, and remember why you are here!" Then we would all gather in a circle and pray as the sun rose. Our prayers would be for those who opposed us, those who supported us from afar, and those who were among us. These prayers continued all day and all night in many forms. In the evening, the sounds of singing and of drums (our mother's heartbeat) could be heard in the dark.[9]

Prayer, ritual, ceremony were everywhere and constant. "The whole time you are in ceremony," said activist AnaYelsi Velasco-Sanchez, who volunteered in the kitchens. "You wake in a space committed to prayer, every action is referred to as an act of prayer. If you are working in the kitchen and you are preparing this food, you are preparing medicine for the people. Prayer was embodied in the space, it was a posture you took."[10]

Predictably, heart-wrenchingly, the militarized police force turned out to protect the interests of the oil business. In the words of one observer who volunteered as a medic:

> . . . ripping elders in the midst of prayer out of sweat lodge, forcing hundreds of people peacefully assembled to strip and stand naked, spraying hundreds of people peacefully assembled with water and chemical weapons in freezing cold weather, barricading the access to advanced healthcare response, blockading the arrival of supplies to keep people healthy and warm in the winter, and shooting sponge grenades and explosive devices at people's faces, groins, and limbs, causing blindness and ripped open flesh.[11]

It was a moment in which the dynamics of today's world surfaced starkly and undeniably: the tension between the interconnected, reverential Native worldview on the one hand, and the violent, exploitative ways of the colonizer on the other.

~~~

If my heart cracked when the camp was broken down, it shattered at the results of the 2016 presidential election. I told Donna, my philanthropy mother, how I just wanted to retreat and avoid white people after that.

She told me that it was a symptom of colonization that I felt that way. And she shared this story:

> Years back, around 1992, I was at the youth and elders gathering at Onondaga. I was in the

cookhouse, the community space—we did every-thing there, shower and hang out and meet as well as, yes, cook and eat—so it was called the cookhouse. It was the end of the gathering, so we were getting ready to leave. We were packing up, and there was an elder sitting at the table with the youth. That's the way learning was done.

I was ready to leave. But then I heard him say, "Europeans coming to this land was not a problem."

As an elder, he had memories of some of the historic activities of [atrocities by] the U.S. government against Native people. So when I heard him say that, I decided I had to stay and listen to him.

"The problem was," he went on, "they forgot their teachings."

I'll never forget that moment. Because it just opened my heart. There are people who remember the teachings, non-Indigenous too. But Indigenous peoples are a living reminder. We're not gone, no matter how many times they tried to make us invisible. We're here as a living reminder. That's what we can be to all institutions, if we're allowed to be.[12]

As Desmond Tutu writes in *The Book of Forgiving*: "When we assault another's humanity, we assault our own humanity. Every person wants to be acknowledged and affirmed for who and what they are, a human being of infinite worth, someone with a place in the world. We can't violate another's dignity without violating our own. Violence, whether in words or deeds, only begets more violence."[13]

It made me remember footage I'd seen of a young woman at Standing Rock. The day after she and her fellow Water Protectors had been gunned down by the militarized police and National Guard using fire hoses and mace and rubber bullets—the very next day—she trudged back to the armed forces with candy in her hands. The Water Protector walked right back up to the same guards and police, moving slowly, her open palms offering the sweets, the way you might approach a feral animal, and she said, *"It's not you, we know it's not your fault, we're not mad at you, we're praying for you."* That young woman was reminding them of a different way to be. *Mitakuye oyasin*—all my relations. We are all related, all connected. The Native way is to bring the oppressor into our circle of healing. Healing cannot occur unless everyone is part of the process. Let it begin.

Notes

Introduction, What If Money Could Heal Us

1. Because this book focuses on race-based disparities, there will not be much if any mention of gender and the wealth of women vs. men. But the dynamics are similar in many ways. The gender wealth gap is far greater than the often-mentioned wage gap (i.e., that women earn 77 to 80 cents for every dollar a man earns on average). Single white women have just 32 cents for every dollar of wealth that single men do. "The disparity is much greater for single women of color, who have only pennies on the dollar compared to single white men." Diana Farrell and Karen Persichilli Keogh, "The Gender Wage Gap Gets a Lot of Attention, but Another Metric Is Even More Disconcerting," *Business Insider*, May 15, 2017, http://www .businessinsider.de/jpmorgan-on-gender-wealth-gap-2017-5.

The top 25 richest people in the U.S. on the 2016 *Forbes* 400 had a combined net worth of over $900 billion and are all white. Of them, Alice Walton (13th place), Jacqueline Mars (16th place, sharing it with her husband John Mars, yes, like the candy), and Laurene Powell Jobs (23rd place) are the only women. Of the next 25 places, 23 are occupied by white men, the remaining two by white women. Chase Peterson-Withorn, "Forbes 400: The Full List of the Richest People in America 2016," *Forbes*, October 4, 2016, https://www.forbes .com/sites/chasewithorn/2016/10/04/forbes-400-the-full-list-of-the-richest-people-in-america-2016/.

As for the people working in financial services (banking, insurance, asset management, and professional services firms like Deloitte and PWC), only one in four of those who reach a senior role is female, according to a 2017 study by the *Financial Times*. Laura Noonan, Alan Smith, David Blood, and Martin Stabe, "Women Still Miss Out on Management in Finance," *Financial Times*, April 4, 2017, https://ig.ft.com/managements-missing-women-data/.

2. Ken Stern, "Why the Rich Don't Give to Charity," *The Atlantic*, April 2013, https://www.theatlantic.com/magazine/archive/2013/04/why-the-rich-dont-give/309254/.

3. D5 Coalition, *State of the Work*, April 2016, p. 8.

4. BoardSource, "Foundation Board Leadership: A Closer Look at Board Responses to 'Leading with Intent 2017,'" (Washington, DC: BoardSource, 2017), 17.

5. Data refers to grants that explicitly target specific communities of color; obviously a wide range of grantmaking on issues can impact people of color as well. Rick Cohen, "Data Snapshot on Racial Justice Grantmaking," *Philanthropic Initiative for Racial Equity: Critical Issues* 5 (June 2014): 38.

6. Patrick Caldwell, "The Financial Industry Doesn't Want You to Know about its Lack of Diversity," *Mother Jones*, March 11, 2014, https://www.motherjones.com/politics/2014/03/financial-firm-diversity-jobs/.

7. Scott Austin, "White Men Still Dominate the Venture Industry," *Wall Street Journal*, November 21, 2011, https://blogs.wsj.com/venturecapital/2011/11/21/venture-industry-still-dominated-by-white-males-survey/.

8. Brian Solomon, "White Males Still Dominate the $23 Billion Angel Investing Community," *Forbes*, November 25, 2014, https://www.forbes.com/sites/brian solomon/2014/11/25/white-males-still-dominate-the-23-billion-angel-investing-community-infographic/.

9. Minority Business Development Agency, U.S. Department of Commerce, 2010. Cited in Anita Li, "The Black Entrepreneur Trying to End Startup Racism is Almost Out of Cash," Mashable, July 21, 2014, https://mashable.com/2014/07/21/startup-racism/.

10. CB Insights, "Venture Capital Human Capital Report," August 3, 2010, https://www.cbinsights.com/research/venture-capital-human-capital-report/.

11. Malcolm X, "The Harlem 'Hate-Gang' Scare," in *Malcolm X Speaks* (New York: Pathfinder, 1989), 68–69. Answer to a question during the question period following his speech at the Militant Labor Forum held in New York on May 29, 1964.

12. David Graeber, *Debt: The First 5,000 Years* (New York: Melville House, 2011), 47.

Part One, Where It Hurts

1. Audre Lorde, essay with this title in *Sister Outsider* (Berkeley: Ten Speed Press, 1984).

Chapter One, Stolen and Sold

1. Renee Danielle Singh, "Our Roots Go Back to Roanoke: Investigating the Link between the Lost Colony and the Lumbee People of North Carolina," student paper, University of California, Davis, 2006. Also see Malinda Maynor Lowery, *Lumbee Indians in the Jim Crow South* (Chapel Hill: University of North Carolina Press, 2010).

2. Priscilla Long, "Duwamish Tribe Wins Federal Recognition on January 19, 2001, but Loses It Again Two Days Later," HistoryLink.org, January 20, 2001, http://www.historylink.org/File/2951.

3. Shall I recommend some? *An Indigenous Peoples' History of the United States*, by Roxanne Dunbar-Ortiz. *The Origin of Others*, by Toni Morrison. *Racecraft: The Soul of Equality in American Life*, by Barbara E. Fields and Karen J. Fields. *Sacred Economics: Money, Gift, and Society in the Age of Transition*, by Charles Eisenstein.

4. Derek Rasmussen, "Reweaving our Social Fabric and Stemming the Tide of De-indigenization," plenary talk at the Economics of Happiness conference, Portland, Oregon, February 2015. https://www.youtube.com/watch?v=cr87shQNnYA.

5. Robin DiAngelo, "No, I Won't Stop Saying 'White Supremacy,'" *YES!* magazine, June 30, 2017, http://www.yesmagazine.org/people-power/no-i-wont-stop-say ing-white-supremacy-20170630.

6. Ibid.

7. Vanessa Daniel, "America Is Burning," Medium, September 13, 2017, https://medium.com/@GroundswellFund/americaisburning-4f154e201a3a.

8. DiAngelo, "No, I Won't Stop Saying 'White Supremacy.'"

9. Jon Stone, "British people Are Proud of Colonialism and the British Empire, Poll Finds," *The Independent*, January 19, 2016, http://www.independent.co.uk/news/uk/politics/british-people-are-proud-of-colonialism-and-the-british-empire-poll-finds-a6821206.html.

10. YouGov UK, "The British Empire Is 'Something to Be Proud Of,'" July 26, 2014, https://yougov.co.uk/news/2014/07/26/britain-proud-its-empire/.

11. Albert Memmi, *The Colonizer and the Colonized* (New York: Viking Adult, 1965), 64. Emphasis added.

12. National Congress of American Indians, "Indian Country Demographics," citing 2010 U.S. Census, http://www.ncai.org/about-tribes/demographics (accessed April 2018).

13. $38,530 was the median household income of Native households in 2015, compared with $55,775 for the nation as a whole. Data from the 2015 American Community Survey, cited by Levi Rickert, "U.S. Census Bureau: Native American Statistics," Native News Online, November 24, 2016, https://nativenewsonline.net/currents/u-s-census-bureau-native-american-statistics/.

14. The dropout rate for Natives is 30 percent (47 percent for those in Bureau of Indian Education schools) versus the national dropout average of 18 percent. A more jarring statistic: while more than 60 percent of average high school students go on to college, only 17 percent of

Natives continue to college. Helen Oliff, "Graduation Rates and American Indian Education," Partnership with Native Americans, May 16, 2017, http://blog.nativepartnership.org/graduation-rates-american-indian-education/.

15. Centers for Disease Control and Prevention's National Center for Health Statistics, National Vital Statistics System Mortality Data 2012–2013, http://wonder.cdc.gov/ucd-icd10.html.

16. Emily Erasim and Osprey Orielle Lake, "Women on the Front Lines Fighting Fracking in the Bakken Oil Shale Formations," citing U.S. Department of Justice records, EcoWatch, March 12, 2016, http://ecowatch.com/2016/03/12/women-frontlines-fighting-fracking/.

17. Kenrya Rankin, "Report: Juvenile Justice System Is Failing Native Youth," Colorlines, August 3, 2015, http://www.colorlines.com/articles/report-juvenile-justice-system-failing-native-youth.

18. "Disparities Factsheet," Indian Health Service, https://www.ihs.gov/newsroom/factsheets/disparities/ (accessed April 2018).

19. "Health Disparities in UIHO Service Areas Factsheet," Urban Indian Health Institute, http://www.uihi.org/wp-content/uploads/2017/08/UIHO_Fact-Sheet_20150227.pdf.

20. Dan Hurley, "Grandma's Experiences Leave Mark on Your Genes," Discover, May 2013, http://discovermagazine.com/2013/may/13-grandmas-experiences-leave-epigenetic-mark-on-your-genes.

21. Frantz Fanon, The Wretched of the Earth (New York: Grove Press, 1964), 36.

22. Delilah Friedler, "Indigenous Land Acknowledgement, Explained," Teen Vogue, February 8, 2018, https://www.teenvogue.com/story/indigenous-land-acknowledgement-explained.

Chapter Two, Arriving at the Plantation

1. Reynolds history from author's experiences, supplement with information from the book by Patrick Reynolds and Tom Schachtman, *The Gilded Leaf: Triumph, Tragedy, and Tobacco: Three Generations of the R. J. Reynolds Family and Fortune* (Boston: Little, Brown, 1989).

2. Anonymous, interview by the author, July 18, 2017.

3. Anonymous, interview by the author, July 23, 2017.

4. Jess Rimington and Joanna Levitt Cea, "Decolonizing Design," September 2016, draft shared with the author, from the forthcoming book *The Recollective Way.*

5. Kenneth Jones and Tema Okun, "White Supremacy Culture," *Dismantling Racism* (ChangeWork, 2001), http://www.cwsworkshop.org/PARC_site_B/dr-culture.html (accessed May 2018).

Chapter 3, House Slaves

1. Anonymous, interview by the author, July 10, 2017.

2. Anonymous, interview by the author, April 10, 2017.

3. Ibid.

4. Anonymous, interview by the author, July 18, 2017.

5. Anonymous, interview by the author, April 10, 2017.

6. Anonymous, interview by the author, April 12, 2017.

7. Anonymous, interview by the author, July 26, 2017.

8. Anonymous, interview by the author, July 20, 2017.

9. Anonymous, interview by the author, July 18, 2017.

10. D5 Coalition, *Foundations Facilitate Diversity, Equity and Inclusion*, September 2, 2014, http://www.d5coalition.org/wp-content/uploads/2014/08/D5_OMGreport_072814-1.pdf, p. 8.

11. Anonymous, interview by the author, April 12, 2017.

12. LM Strategies on behalf of ABFE, "The Exit Interview," May 2014, http://www.abfe.org/wp-content/uploads/2014/05/ABFE-The-Exit-Interview.pdf.

13. Anonymous, interview by the author, July 20, 2017.

14. Courtney Martin, "The Trouble with Philanthropy Is that Money Can't Buy Equality," *The Guardian*, September 2, 2016, https://www.theguardian.com/global-development-professionals-network/2016/sep/02/philanthropists-revolution-libraries-grassroots.

15. D5 Coalition, *State of the Work Year Five*, April 2016, http://www.d5coalition.org/wp-content/uploads/2016/04/D5-SOTW-2016-Final-web-pages.pdf, p. 7.

16. Ibid.

17. Gara LaMarche, "Democracy and the Donor Class," *Democracy* 34 (Fall 2014), https://democracyjournal.org/magazine/34/democracy-and-the-donor-class/.

18. Patrick Caldwell, "The Financial Industry Doesn't Want You to Know about its Lack of Diversity," *Mother Jones*, March 11, 2014, https://www.motherjones.com/politics/2014/03/financial-firm-diversity-jobs/.

19. CB Insights, "Venture Capital Human Capital Report," August 3, 2010, https://www.cbinsights.com/research/venture-capital-human-capital-report%20.

20. Robert W. Fairlie, Ph.D., and Alicia M. Robb, Ph.D., *Disparities in Capital Access between Minority and Non-Minority-Owned Businesses*, Minority Business Development Agency, U.S. Department of Commerce, January 2010, https://people.ucsc.edu/~rfairlie/presentations/Disparities%20in%20Capital%20Access%20Report%202010.pdf.

21. Michael A. Cohen, Maria Figueroa Küpçü, and Parag Khanna, "The New Colonialists," *Foreign Policy* (November–December 2008), reprinted online in the *Utne Reader*, http://www.utne.com/politics/the-new-colonialists.

22. Caldwell, "The Financial Industry Doesn't Want You to Know about its Lack of Diversity."

23. Vu Le, "Are You Guilty of Fakequity? If So, What to Do About It," Nonprofit AF, http://nonprofitaf.com/2015/03/are-you-guilty-of-fakequity-if-so-what-to-do-about-it/ (accessed May 2018).

24. Anonymous, interview by the author, July 26, 2017.

25. Anonymous, interview by the author, August 14, 2017.

26. Anonymous, interview by the author, July 10, 2017.

27. Floyd Mills, "State of Change" Report, July 27, 2017, Council on Foundations. See also the article by Mark Hrywna, "Little Progress on Staff, Executive Diversity," *NonProfit Times*, July 28, 2017, http://www.thenonprofittimes.com/news-articles/little-progress-diversity-staff/.

28. Frank Dobbin and Alexandra Kalev, "Why Diversity Programs Fail," *Harvard Business Review* (July–August 2016), https://hbr.org/2016/07/why-diversity-programs-fail.

29. Andrea Armeni, interview by author, December 18, 2017.

30. Chris Cardona, interview by author, June 15, 2017.

31. Ryan Bowers, interview by author, December 10, 2017.

Chapter Four, Field Hands

1. Chris Cardona, interview by author, June 15, 2017.

2. Anonymous, interview by author, July 1, 2017.

3. adrienne maree brown, *Emergent Strategy: Shaping Change, Changing Worlds* (Oakland: AK Press, 2017).

4. Vu Le, "In the Trump Era, Nonprofits Need a New Social Contract with Foundations," Philanthropy.com, November 14, 2016, https://www.philanthropy.com/article/Opinion-In-the-Trump-Era/238408.

5. Anonymous, interview by author, July 15, 2017.

6. Will Pittz and Rinku Sen, *Short Changed: Foundation Giving and Communities of Color*, Applied Research Center, Spring 2004, http://www.racialequitytools.org/resourcefiles/pitz.pdf.

7. Rick Cohen, "Data Snapshot on Racial Justice Grantmaking," *Philanthropic Initiative for Racial Equity: Critical Issues* 5 (June 2014), http://racialequity.org/docs/CIF5.pdf.

8. Lawrence T. McGill, Brielle Bryan, and Eugene D. Miller, *Benchmarking Diversity: A First Look at New York City Foundations and Nonprofits*, Foundation Center, 2009, https://philanthropynewyork.org/sites/default/files/resources/Benchmarking%20Diversity_NYC%20Foundations%20and%20Nonprofits.PDF (accessed May 2018).

9. Robert W. Fairlie, Ph.D., and Alicia M. Robb, Ph.D., *Disparities in Capital Access between Minority and Non-Minority-Owned Businesses*, Minority Business Development Agency, U.S. Department of Commerce, January 2010, https://people.ucsc.edu/~rfairlie/presentations/Disparities%20in%20Capital%20Access%20Report%202010.pdf.

10. Note from Jessica Norwood, November 13, 2016. See also http://www.therunwayproject.org.

11. Note from Jessica Norwood, November 13, 2016.

12. CB Insights, "Venture Capital Human Capital Report," August 3, 2010, https://www.cbinsights.com/research/venture-capital-human-capital-report%20.

13. Anonymous, interview by author, December 10, 2017.

14. Debbie Gruentstein Bocian, Wei Li, and Keith Ernst, "Foreclosures by Race and Ethnicity: The Demographics of a Crisis," Center for Responsible Lending, June 18, 2010, http://www.responsiblelending.org/mortgage-lending/research-analysis/foreclosures-by-race-and-ethnicity.pdf.

15. Ryan Bowers, interview by author, December 12, 2017.

16. Ibid.

Chapter Five, The Overseers

1. Terrance Keenan, *The Promise at Hand: Prospects for Foundation Leadership in the 1990s*, Robert Wood Johnson Foundation, 1992. Available to download in full: http://www.policyarchive.org/handle/10207/21820.

2. "Terrance Keenan obituary," *New York Times*, March 7, 2009.

3. Paul Lukas, "UPS United Parcel Service James Casey Transformed a Tiny Messenger Service into the World's Largest Shipper by Getting All Wrapped Up in the Details of Package Delivery," CNN Money, April 1, 2003, http://money.cnn.com/magazines/fsb/fsb_archive/2003/04/01/341024/.

4. Martin Luther King, Jr., "Where Do We Go from Here?" speech delivered at the Southern Christian Leadership Conference, Atlanta, GA, August 16, 1967.

Chapter Six, Freedom

1. adrienne maree brown, *Emergent Strategy* (Oakland: AK Press, 2017).

2. Donna Chavis, interview by author, August 17, 2017.

3. Ibid.

4. Ibid.

5. Gabor Maté, interview by Jenara Nerenberg, "Why Are So Many Adults Haunted by Trauma?" *Greater Good Magazine*, June 8, 2017, https://greatergood.berkeley.edu/article/item/why_are_so_many_adults_today_haunted_by_trauma.

Part Two, How to Heal

1. Peter Block, *Community: The Structure of Belonging* (Oakland: Berrett-Koehler, 2008).

Step One, Grieve

1. Stephen Jenkinson, "Orphan Wisdom," https://orphanwisdom.com/about/ (accessed May 2018). Please don't miss his important, gorgeous book *Die Wise* (Berkeley: North Atlantic Books, 2015)

2. Aurora Levins Morales, *Medicine Stories* (Boston: South End Press, 1999).

3. Hilary Giovale, interview by author, August 20, 2017.

4. Ibid.

5. Peter Buffett, interview by author, December 10, 2017.

6. Mias deKlerk. "Healing Emotional Trauma in Organizations: An O.D. Framework and Case Study," *Organization Development Journal* 25 (Summer 2007).

7. Bourree Lam, "The Fear of Feelings at Work," *The Atlantic*, May 1, 2017, https://www.theatlantic.com/business/archive/2017/05/feelings-at-work/524970/.

Step Two, Apologize

1. Pumla Gobodo-Madikizela, *A Human Being Died that Night* (Mariner Books, 2004).

2. "Apology to Australia's Indigenous Peoples," February 13, 2008, https://www.australia.gov.au/about-australia/our-country/our-people/apology-to-australias-indigenous-peoples.

3. "About the National Centre for Truth and Reconciliation," http://nctr.ca/about-new.php (accessed May 2018).

4. Rob Capriccioso, "A Sorry Saga: Obama Signs Native American Apology Resolution; Fails to Draw Attention to It," Indian Law Resource Center, January 13, 2010, http://indianlaw.org/node/529.

5. Ibid.

6. "The Empire Pays Back," 2005, available to watch in full online at https://www.youtube.com/watch?v=MzctBXOHewk.

7. Peter Buffett, "Magic Words," https://www.peterbuffett.com/written-reflections/magic-words (accessed May 2018).

8. Hilary Giovale, interview by author, August 20, 2017.

9. Edward J. Blum, *W. E. B. Du Bois, American Prophet* (Philadelphia: University of Pennsylvania Press, 2009).

10. "The Philanthropic Community's Declaration of Action," available to download in full at http://www.philanthropyandaboriginalpeoples.ca/wp-content/uploads/DECLARATION-TRC-English-FINAL-20150527-355pm.pdf.

12. Sarah Lyons, interview by author, June 18, 2017.

Step Three, Listen

1. Jennifer and Peter Buffett, interview by author, December 10, 2017.

2. Amber Nystrom, "How to Shut Up, and Other Lessons from the Godfather of Impact Investing—Jed Emerson," *Conscious Company* 10 (November/December 2016), http://greenmoneyjournal.com/how-to-shut-up-and-other-lessons-from-the-godfather-of-impact-investing-jed-emerson/.

3. Otto Scharmer and Katrin Kaufer, *Leading from the Emerging Future* (Oakland: Berrett-Koehler Publishers, 2013).

Step Four, Relate

1. Christopher Alexander, *The Timeless Way of Building* (Oxford: Oxford University Press, 1979).

2. Christopher Alexander, *The Luminous Ground: The Nature of Order, Book 4* (London: Routledge, 2004).

3. Pamela Shifman, interview by author, August 10, 2017.

4. Ibid.

5. Yasmin Anwar, "Creating Love in the Lab: The 36 Questions that Spark Intimacy," *Berkeley News*, February 12, 2015, http://news.berkeley.edu/2015/02/12/love-in-the-lab/.

6. Jennifer and Peter Buffett, interview by author, December 10, 2017.

7. Jeremy Heimans and Henry Timms, "Understanding 'New Power,'" *Harvard Business Review* (December 2014), https://hbr.org/2014/12/understanding-new-power.

8. Frederic Laloux, *Reinventing Organizations* (Brussels: Nelson Parker, 2014).

Step Five, Represent

1. Daryn Dodson, interview by author, December 3, 2017.

2. Bryan Stevenson, lecture at Yale Divinity School, February 1, 2017.

3. Gara LaMarche, interview by author, August 15, 2017.

4. Nevin Öztop, interview by author, August 3, 2017.

5. Pamela Shifman, interview by author, August 10, 2017.

6. "Neighborhood Strength: Creating a New Grant-making Model in Crown Heights Brooklyn," Brooklyn Community Foundation, http://neighborhoods.brooklyncommunityfoundation.org/ (accessed May 2018).

7. Anna Clark, "Is Participatory Budgeting Real Democracy?" Next City, April 28, 2014, https://nextcity.org/features/view/is-participatory-budgeting-real-democracy-chicago.

8. Ibid.

9. Jordan Flaherty, *No More Heroes: Grassroots Challenges to the Savior Mentality* (Oakland: AK Press, 2016).

10. Caitlin Breedlove, "Willing to Be Transformed," Medium, September 24, 2015, https://medium.com/@caitlinbreedlove/willing-to-be-transformed-a-nine-year-queer-cross-race-work-marriage-33dd247d0bd5.

11. "Beyond Political Correctness: Building a Diverse Board," BoardSource, https://www.bridgespan.org/insights/library/boards/building-a-diverse-board (accessed May 2018).

12. Phillip Jackson, interview by author, August 26, 2017.

Step Six, Invest

1. Dana Arviso, interview by author, May 26, 2017.

2. Gregory Gethard, "Protest Divestment and the End of Apartheid," *Investopedia*, https://www.investopedia.com/articles/economics/08/protest-divestment-south-africa.asp (accessed May 2018).

3. Darren Walker, "Unleashing the Power of Endowments: The Next Great Challenge for Philanthropy," Ford Foundation, April 5, 2017, https://www.fordfoundation.org/ideas/equals-change-blog/posts/unleashing-the-power-of-endowments-the-next-great-challenge-for-philanthropy/.

4. "The Evolution of Heron," F. B. Heron Foundation, http://www.heron.org/enterprise (accessed May 2018).

5. Ibid.

6. F. B. Heron Investment Policy Statement, December 5, 2016, available to download in full at http://www.heron.org/engage/publications/investment-policy-statement.

7. Amy Cortese, "For Impact Investor Kristin Hull, There Are Many Ways to Effect Change," Locavesting, May 19, 2017, https://www.locavesting.com/investing/for-impact-investor-kristin-hull-there-are-many-ways-to-effect-change/.

8. Ibid.

9. Vanessa Daniel, "America Is Burning," Medium, September 13, 2017, https://medium.com/@GroundswellFund/americaisburning-4f154e201a3a.

Step Seven, Repair

1. PwC press release, Global Assets under Management Set to Rise to $145.4 Trillion by 2025, https://press.pwc.com/News-releases/global-assets-under-management-set-to-rise-to--145.4-trillion-by-2025/s/e236a113-5115-4421-9c75-77191733f15f.

2. Rick Cohen, "Data Snapshot on Racial Justice Grant making," *Philanthropic Initiative for Racial Equity: Critical Issues 5* (June 2014): 38.

3. Phillip Jackson, interview by author, August 26, 2017.

4. According to the US SIF Foundation's 2016 *Report on US Sustainable, Responsible and Impact Investing Trends*, as of year-end 2015, more than one out of every five dollars under professional management in the United States—$8.72 trillion or more—was invested according to SRI strategies.

5. Richard F. America, "Reparations and Higher Education," *Diverse Issues in Higher Education*, January 7, 1999, http://diverseeducation.com/article/16/.

6. Ta-Nehisi Coates, "The Case for Reparations," *The Atlantic*, June 2014, https://www.theatlantic.com/magazine/archive/2014/06/the-case-for-reparations/361631/.

7. "Two Economies," Movement New Lab, https://movementnetlab.org/living-resource-systems-a-new-approach-for-supporting-movement-networks/ (accessed May 2018).

8. Adam Simpson, Carla Skandier, and William A. Darity, Jr., "For Reparations," the Next System Project, March 10, 2017, https://thenextsystem.org/for-reparations.

9. Robert Pollin, James Heintz, and Thomas Herndon, "The Revenue Potential of a Financial Transaction Tax for U.S. Financial Markets," Political Economy Research Insti-tute, University of Massachusetts at Amherst, July 30, 2017, https://www.peri.umass.edu/publication/item/698-the-revenue-potential-of-a-financial-transaction-tax-for-u-s-financial-markets.

10. Naomi Schaefer Riley, "One Way to Help Native Americans: Property Rights," *The Atlantic*, July 30, 2016, https://www.theatlantic.com/politics/archive/2016/07/native-americans-property-rights/492941/.

11. Simpson, Skandier, and Darity, "For Reparations."

Conclusion, Coming Full Circle

1. adrienne maree brown, *Emergent Strategy: Shaping Change, Changing Worlds* (Oakland: AK Press, 2017).

2. Donna Chavis, interview by author, August 17, 2017.

3. Ibid.

4. Ibid.

5. Dana Arviso, interview by author, May 26, 2017.

6. David Graeber "Army of Altruists," *Harper's*, January 2007, https://harpers.org/archive/2007/01/army-of-altruists/.

7. Robin Wall Kimmerer, *Braiding Sweetgrass: Indigenous Wisdom, Scientific Knowledge and the Teachings of Plants* (Minneapolis: Milkweed Editions, 2013), 165.

8. Iyuskin American Horse, "'We Are Protectors, not Protesters': Why I'm Fighting the North Dakota Pipeline," *Guardian UK*, August 18, 2016, https://www.theguardian.com/us-news/2016/aug/18/north-dakota-pipeline-activists-bakken-oil-fields.

9. Camille Seaman, "Gallery: Portraits from the Standing Rock Protests," Ideas.TED.com, November 9, 2016, https://ideas.ted.com/gallery-portraits-from-the-standing-rock-protests/.

10. Morgan Guyton, "Decolonizing Christianity with Alicia Crosby and AnaYelsi Velasco-Sanchez," Crackers and Grape Juice podcast, Episode 61, posted on Patheos, December 13, 2016, http://www.patheos.com/blogs/mercynotsacrifice/2016/12/13/ decolonizing-christianity-alicia-crosby-anayelsi-velasco-sanchez/.

11. Dr. Rupa Marya, Facebook post, Spring 2016.

12. Donna Chavis, interview by author, August 17, 2017.

13. Desmond Tutu, *The Book of Forgiving* (San Francisco: HarperOne, 2014).

Glossary of
New Terms

colonizer virus: What remains in society, culture, and institutions after the conquest phase of colonization is done, compelling tactics of division, control, and exploitation. Nowhere is the virus more present than in how we deal with wealth.

global bleaching: The side effect of colonizers traveling the earth to consolidate wealth: a staggering reduction in the number of religions, languages, species, cultures, social systems, media channels, political systems, etc. The result is a more bland and boring world that is less innovative and less resilient.

ivory towers: Institutions that maintain the white supremacist culture and operate according to the colonizer mantra of *divide, control, exploit*.

listening in color: The combination of listening openly without controlling the parameters of what can be said; listening with empathy and allowing the experiences of the speaker to permeate; and listening for what is being said beyond the words spoken.

loans-to-gifts spectrum: The collection of institutions that control access to wealth, from banks to investment firms to foundations, collectively also called funders.

medicine money: Resources and wealth used intentionally to heal divides and restore balance to the earth.

orphans: A compassionate term for non-Indigenous people of all backgrounds, indicating the severing from their ancestral territories and their ancient ways (with thanks to Stephen Jenkinson).

shiny new penny syndrome: An aspect of internalized oppression, when a new person of color threatens the existing token person of color's position of power.

Whitney Houston–Bobby Brown syndrome: An aspect of internalized oppression in which you have to diminish yourself in order to not steal the spotlight of someone else at your organization who has more power than you.

Acknowledgements

Thanks to the Creator and to my sweet mother, Sheila Jacobs Whaley. Thanks, Momma, for your unconditional love and for teaching me the spirit of giving and generosity of the heart. And to the rest of my family, thank you for always finding a good laugh even in the face of adversity. I love you.

Eternal gratitude to my chosen family—the loves of my life and my soul mates—for your support during this project and in life in general: Will Cordery, Mayra Alvarez Sparacino, Sadye Paez, Michelle Ramos Lopez, Yesenia Polanco, Chris Locklear, Tenney Farmer, and Buddy.

The following foundations provided support for the writing of this book:

Arcus Foundation, California Wellness Foundation, Ford Foundation, Geo Family Foundation, Robert Sterling Clark Foundation, Schott Foundation for Public Education, and The Solutions Project. Thank you for leading the way in reimaging transformational philanthropy.

The following philanthropists, funders, advocates, Indigenous leaders, and all-around good folks provided insights and wisdom to this work:

Andrea Armeni, Dana Arviso, Tamieka Atkins, Ryan Bowers, Kelly Brown, Jennifer and Peter Buffett, David Callahan, Chris Cardona,

Acknowledgements / 202

Anges Chavis, Donna Chavis, William Cordery, Aaron Dorfman, Sarah Eagle Heart, Farhad A. Ebrahimi, Kwabena Allen Frimpong, Jose A. Garcia, Hilary Giovale, Gita Gulati-Partee, Carly Hare, Phillip Jackson, Melissa Johnson, Elizabeth Krause, Gara LaMarche, Melinda Maynor Lowery, Tyler Nickerson, Sarah Lyons, Nevin Öztop, Leticia Peguero, Tia Oros Peters, Cynthia Renfro, Pamela Shifman, Christi Tran, and Dorian Warren.

Thanks also to:

- The staff and board of Native Americans in Philanthropy for being a committed partner in advocating for investment in Native communities.
- My Schott Foundation colleagues for trusting me and supporting my leadership.
- Karen McNeil Miller for taking a chance on me by giving me my first gig in philanthropy and for shaping my worldview about the field of philanthropy.
- Ai-jen Poo for inspiration in so many ways and for introducing me to Ariane.
- Hilary Giovale for being the first white person to ever apologize to me for the transgressions of your ancestors and for being a living example of transformation.
- My Rockwood Leadership cohort who pushed me to take this step, then went above and beyond to make it a reality, especially you, Phil Li. Akaya Windwood, thank you for pushing me to have

that "conversation you are not having" and for introducing me to my editor.

- Kevin Jennings for being my hero in so many ways.
- The team at Berrett-Koehler Publishers, especially my editor Steve Piersanti, who have been a huge cheerleader from the start of our relationship.
- Native Youth—all of you—for your resilience and power which give me hope every day. You are my inspiration to do this work.
- The Lumbee Tribe of North Carolina—my people—for keeping me grounded. Healing is our path to a better life.

To my philanthropic elders—the leaders of color who came before me and coached and loved me—I stand on your shoulders: Susan Taylor Batten, Angela Glover Blackwell, Donna Chavis, Louis Delgado, Linetta Gilbert, Susan Jenkins, Valorie Johnson, Peggy Saika, Gladys Washington, to name a few.

To everyone who has worked with me in any way—I'm better off because of you. There are too many names to list, but thank you.

Last but not least, Ariane Conrad, the Book Doula and so much more. You are the most brilliant (and patient) person I've ever met. My life is forever changed because of you.

Index

About the Author

From an early age, Edgar Villanueva knew he would devote himself to ministry, to medicine, to being of service. He earned a bachelor of arts degree from Jackson College of Ministries, and a bachelor of science in public health and a master's degree in health administration from the University of North Carolina's Gillings Global School of Public Health. Ultimately, he found his way to philanthropy, the field named for the love of humankind, where for the past 14 years he has given away tens of millions of dollars each year, mostly to low-income communities across the United States.

This is someone who grew up in extreme poverty, with a valiant single mother determined to see her son get the education that would change his circumstances. Today, Edgar is an executive at a national foundation and serves as the chair of the Board of Native Americans in Philanthropy. He also advises high-net-worth individuals, philanthropists, and funding institutions in allocating resources more equitably. In other words, Edgar is intimately familiar with both sides of the wealth divide.

Edgar is proud to be an enrolled member of the Lumbee Tribe of North Carolina as well as a Southerner, lineages from which he inherited the love of storytelling and his strong devotion to community. His Native name,

Niigaanii Beneshi (Ojibwe), means Leading Bird, signifying the bird at the front of the flock when it flies in V-formation, the bird that bears the full brunt of the wind and sets the pace for the rest. Much of the inspiration for the "medicine" prescribed in the pages of *Decolonizing Wealth* comes from Native elders and the Indigenous worldview.

Like most Lumbee Indians, faith has been a major influence on Edgar's life. The church gave Edgar's early years a stability and purpose that he firmly believes is the reason why he's made it as far as he has. Over the years, his faith has evolved but not wavered. He holds fast to traditions he believes to be valuable.

His chosen family includes the advocates and activists who are engaged in the struggle for racial justice, civil rights, and human rights. They celebrate birthdays and weddings together; they comfort each other in the face of violence and bigotry. Their professional is their personal.

Poverty and wealth; Native, Southern, and Christian traditions; ministry, health care, activism, and philanthropy. Braiding these many threads together gives Edgar his unique perspective on decolonization, the process of recovering from trauma, and the potential for money to help humanity heal.

A frequent presenter at conferences on philanthropy and social finance, where he regularly inspires funders to engage in the Seven Steps to Healing, Edgar is also an instructor at the Grantmaking School at the Johnson Center at Grand Valley State University. He has held leadership roles on numerous boards and advisory committees, including the Andrus Family Fund, the Executives' Alliance to Expand Opportunities for Boys and Men of Color and the Robert Wood Johnson Foundation's Forward Promise National Advisory

Committee. Edgar has been a Hull Fellow with the Southeastern Council of Foundations and a Fellow with the American College of Health Care Executives.

In 2010, he was selected for the inaugural class of the Terrance Keenan Institute for Emerging Leaders in Health Philanthropy fellowship program, designed to cultivate the next generation of philanthropic leadership. In June 2014, Edgar was awarded the Flying Eagle Woman Award from Native Americans in Philanthropy, recognizing his many years in community-led, culturally inspired leadership. It was an apt recognition of the Leading Bird.

Berrett–Koehler
BK Publishers

Berrett-Koehler is an independent publisher dedicated to an ambitious mission: *Connecting people and ideas to create a world that works for all.*

We believe that the solutions to the world's problems will come from all of us, working at all levels: in our organizations, in our society, and in our own lives. Our BK Business books help people make their organizations more humane, democratic, diverse, and effective (we don't think there's any contradiction there). Our BK Currents books offer pathways to creating a more just, equitable, and sustainable society. Our BK Life books help people create positive change in their lives and align their personal practices with their aspirations for a better world.

All of our books are designed to bring people seeking positive change together around the ideas that empower them to see and shape the world in a new way.

And we strive to practice what we preach. At the core of our approach is Stewardship, a deep sense of responsibility to administer the company for the benefit of all of our stakeholder groups including authors, customers, employees, investors, service providers, and the communities and environment around us. Everything we do is built around this and our other key values of quality, partnership, inclusion, and sustainability.

This is why we are both a B-Corporation and a California Benefit Corporation—a certification and a for-profit legal status that require us to adhere to the highest standards for corporate, social, and environmental performance.

We are grateful to our readers, authors, and other friends of the company who consider themselves to be part of the BK Community. We hope that you, too, will join us in our mission.

A BK Currents Book

BK Currents books bring people together to advance social and economic justice, shared prosperity, sustainability, and new solutions for national and global issues. They advocate for systemic change and provide the ideas and tools to solve social problems at their root. So get to it!

To find out more, visit **www.bkconnection.com.**

Berrett–Koehler
Publishers

Connecting people and ideas
to create a world that works for all

Dear Reader,

Thank you for picking up this book and joining our worldwide community of Berrett-Koehler readers. We share ideas that bring positive change into people's lives, organizations, and society.

To welcome you, we'd like to offer you a free e-book. You can pick from among twelve of our bestselling books by entering the promotional code **BKP92E** here: http://www.bkconnection.com/welcome.

When you claim your free e-book, we'll also send you a copy of our e-newsletter, the *BK Communiqué*. Although you're free to unsubscribe, there are many benefits to sticking around. In every issue of our newsletter you'll find

• A free e-book
• Tips from famous authors
• Discounts on spotlight titles
• Hilarious insider publishing news
• A chance to win a prize for answering a riddle

Best of all, our readers tell us, "Your newsletter is the only one I actually read." So claim your gift today, and please stay in touch!

Sincerely,

Charlotte Ashlock
Steward of the BK Website

Questions? Comments? Contact me at bkcommunity@bkpub.com.

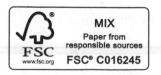

MIX
Paper from
responsible sources
FSC www.fsc.org **FSC® C016245**

Certified

B

Corporation
bcorporation.net